" A well-designed **SPACE** is a well-edited space. I almost always pile things on, only to take away before I'm finished in any room. "

Nate Berkus

Decorate

'Your surroundings and what
you do with them are a vital
part of living.'

Shannon Fricke, stylist

Holly Becker &
Joanna Copestick

Decorate

1,000 inspirational design ideas for every room in your house

Photography by
Debi Treloar

jacqui
small

PRETTY IN PINK
This page Yvonne Eijkenduijn's work space is minimal yet comfortable, with good use of a few key elements, and soft pink and warm white.

UNIFORM COLLECTION
Previous pages Create a display using a collection of identical objects in different sizes. The variety of scale forms a perfect visual harmony.

BLUES AND GREENS
Page 1 Arrange collections of glass close to a natural light source to enjoy their full beauty.

First published in 2011
This edition first published in 2017 by Jacqui Small
An imprint of The Quarto Group
74-77 White Lion Street
London N1 9PF

Publisher Jacqui Small
Editor Sian Parkhouse
Location Research
Holly Becker & Claire Limpus
Managing Editor Kerenza Swift
Designer Robin Rout
Production Peter Colley

British Library Cataloguing-in-Publication Data
A catalogue record for this book is available from the British Library.

ISBN 978 1 911127 47 5

Printed and bound in China

2019 2018 2017
10 9 8 7 6 5 4 3 2 1

Quarto Knows

Quarto is the authority on a wide range of topics.

Quarto educates, entertains and enriches the lives of our readers – enthusiasts and lovers of hands-on living.

FSC
www.fsc.org
MIX
Paper from responsible sources
FSC® C016973

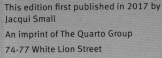

Contents

'Set an inspiration date for yourself. Visit an art gallery. Go window shopping. Spend the afternoon in a book store.' *Carrie McCarthy, author*

'For me home is simply about shelter, in all manners of speaking. It's a place of rest and refuge, a place where I can play, relax, unwind or create – home is the place that replenishes my soul.'

Pia Jane Bijkerk , stylist

"Use your critical eye
to see
and use your heart
to feel —
and then trust your
INSTINCTS."

Shannon Fricke

Introduction

'I want my home to work for me not the
other way around and so every design
choice I make is based on practicality as
well as aesthetics. I really believe a home is
something to live in, not just to admire.'

Atlanta Bartlett , designer

WOODLAND TABLEAU *This page* Simple white wooden shelves decorated with painted tree branches form a witty backdrop for a display of nature-inspired paraphernalia.

STILL LIFE *Previous page* Everyday objects such as china bowls and ceramic plates are often beautiful pieces that merit special attention. Place them together on shelves, windowsills or in cupboards so that they give you pleasure every day.

Decorate

is a different kind of decorating book. Rather than concentrating on one trademark look or a particular design aesthetic, we have concentrated on ideas – more than one thousand of them – to provide fresh insight into how you can transform your home.

Ask any decorator what inspired them to create a space and the answers are extremely varied. For some a painting can trigger a whole colour scheme, for others a piece of quirky retro furniture fuels an eclectic old and new scheme, while many rooms may start from an appreciation of the white space itself – walls, floor and windows. Sometimes the architecture of a space gives a design direction or else a favourite fabric or a trusted paint colour will dictate a country or a modern feel. Learning to see the potential of a dusty cupboard in a flea market or a beautifully framed mirror at an auction, saving up to invest in a key piece of vintage furniture or simply adapting an existing chair or table are all ways of creating room schemes that reflect you and your personal style.

We have asked some of today's most interesting and inspiring creative minds for decorating ideas that reflect a sense of personal style, creativity and confidence at home. Some have opened their style notebooks to provide inspiring ideas; others allowed us to photograph their space where we experienced firsthand how and why their decorating advice truly works; and still others shared recent examples from their professional portfolios, showcasing their talent and innovation. From homes that are quirky to those that are carefully edited, wherever we travelled we gathered insight

'Decorating is an extension of your personal style. Finding your decorating style depends on knowing what you love at a gut level.' *Carrie McCarthy, author*

and wisdom on everything from how to pull together fabulous spaces in all sizes, successful ways to combine colours with finesse, fresh uses of fabrics and wallpaper, how a simple, curated collection can go a long way and much, much more.

Space Matters gives pointers on how to assess what you have and how to work with it, where and when to alter spaces, ideas for how to make a small space feel larger or a dark space lighter and when to allow the architecture itself to dictate the space. Setting Your Style provides advice on how to create your own mood board, using fabric samples, paint swatches and treasured items such as buttons or ribbons as a way of deciding on your own personal style. A number of interior styles, from modern and simple to natural, flea market, eclectic and colourful provide countless ideas to get

you started. Room by Room includes fantastic examples of key rooms in the home, from kitchens and living spaces to bedrooms and bathrooms, work rooms and creative spaces to children's rooms. Throughout, case studies provide detailed information on key homes while room plans give practical guidance on why each space works so well. Finally Attention to Detail outlines the vital finishing touches that can make or break an interior, from china and flowers to soft furnishings.

This book shows easy ways to work with what you have, keeps an eye on the budget and encourages you to see the possibilities from many different starting points and a whole host of styles. Whether you love boho or deco, vintage or retro, country or contemporary, this book provides ideas and interiors to encourage you to be creative and Decorate.

OUTDOORS IN An elegantly unobtrusive coffee table allows the painted concrete floor to reflect the bright natural light and bring the space to life in Amy Neunsinger's Los Angeles home.

"Allow yourself **the patience** to know it will all come together in time **and enjoy the process!** For me home décor is not a goal, but a continually **EVOLVING** and kinetic art project. "

Amy Butler

Space Matters

CITY LIGHT *This page* In a revamped Brooklyn brownstone, Lyndsay Caleo and Fitzhugh Karol renovated without compromising style.

OLD AND NEW *Previous page* Frédéric Méchiche's exquisite choice of chairs and tables furnishes the space without pulling attention away from the architectural detailing.

'When you intentionally decorate the look and feel of your space you become more genuinely yourself, more at home in your skin and in your space.' *Carrie McCarthy, author*

WHITE SPACE THINKING

One of the joys of interior design is to create a space where spending time is a pleasure. Think about rooms that make you feel most at ease. The reason might be obvious, such as a generous light-filled space with big welcoming sofas, or much more subtle – a kitchen where form and function marry together in such a way that the space performs as much as a living area as it does a place of food preparation. Either way, think about what works for you, and why.

Create a personal checklist of what matters to you. If you love the light, then make sure you place furniture close to windows to enjoy the view. If you are always in the kitchen, make sure it is a place where friends can hang out too, and if you enjoy a sense of space, think about banishing the walls in favour of sliding screens or transparent doors.

WHITE SPACE DESIGN involves removing all the elements from your room, either physically or mentally, by drawing up an entirely new floor plan. Whether you wish to discard unloved furniture, ditch the drab drapes or furnish a newly constructed space, the process will throw up new possibilities. Maybe you could install a fireplace or perhaps a new window treatment?

Putting it on paper A room plan allows you to analyze your space and think about how you use the room. Do you want comfort or function to dominate? Are you able to break up the arrangement with room dividers or place furniture to delineate certain areas? Think about amalgamating living and eating areas for a one space approach or, conversely, placing temporary room dividers to create an intimate entertaining room.

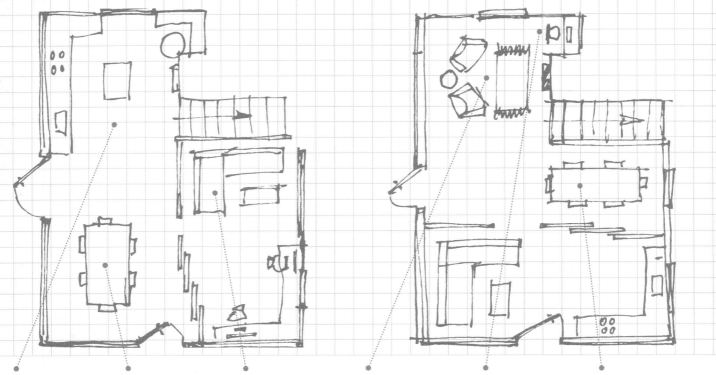

A kitchen/eating area is ideal for families.

Think about the shape of dining table that suits your room.

L-shaped sofas make cosy corners in rectangular spaces.

Create an intimate seating area by placing furniture around a focal point.

One space living enables you to create different zones, such as a home office.

Seating and eating areas close to one another make good socializing spaces.

FRAME YOUR VIEW
Once you have decided
how you want to live in
your space and assessed
a room's best assets you
can start to think about
how to organize the basics
– furniture and window
treatments for instance,
and decoration for walls
and floors.

The Importance of Planning

WORKING WITH WHAT YOU HAVE

Draw up a list of what you have to work with – available light, room plans, furniture, furnishings and accessories.

Decide on whether each space is defined by its function – such as a kitchen or a workspace – or whether it is a place in which you can decorate purely with relaxation in mind.

If your rooms have any particular architectural features such as ceiling cornices, fireplaces, wall panelling or interesting doors, then integrate these into a decorative scheme that allows them to stand out.

Work out how you live in each room. Will you entertain and dine in the kitchen? Will your living room be open to the kitchen and dining area? Do you have children and will they need their own dedicated playspace?

Do you have space in the bedroom for an en-suite bathroom and a dressing area? Or could you create room by knocking through into another room or stealing space from a landing or hallway?

You may need to use furniture you have inherited or invested in, such as a family dining table or an expensive sofa.

Maybe you have a dark space but no budget to install new windows or knock down walls, so you'll need to use pale colours to lighten the space.

Think about what else you possess that may fit into your desired scheme.

GO WITH THE ARCHITECTURE Let the building do the talking and make use of natural focal points such as fireplaces or feature windows. Here a casual seating area either side of the fire is informal and inviting.

SLEEK KITCHEN Compact white units slip neatly into a corner of a high-ceilinged kitchen/diner, where a family blackboard and plenty of storage are useful elements.

ROOM TO VIEW

Creating a double doorway entrance to a room always enhances the space within and allows an enticing view into it. Here large-scale planters and overhead pendants play with scale to dramatic effect.

CLEAN AND WHITE

Pared down simplicity with white marble walls, glass and a dark wood floor works beautifully for walk-in showers and rooms where a sense of space is important.

PUTTING PLANS INTO ACTION

Use your room plans to place all your existing furniture, lighting, rugs and soft furnishings and get a feel for what you have and what you need.

Decide on a ditch list for items that you no longer love or that need to be replaced. Now could be the time for the new dining table you have coveted or an opportunity to make new curtains from your vintage finds.

You need to think about your style and what works with it and whether your home reflects that style or dictates a certain design direction of its own.

If your room is bland and box-like, work out how to incorporate an interesting focal point. Maybe a mantel shelf for display, a large piece of freestanding furniture or a stunning piece of art to take up one wall.

Use colour to define the space by painting one wall a different colour or using wallpaper as a focal point.

Lighting can be dramatic if you choose a huge chandelier, either bespoke or ready-made.

Flooring is important, too. Stripped or painted wood? Carpet or rugs? Industrial concrete or smart linoleum?

Now's the time to innovate. Make a display of your shoe collection, find space for your favourite capsule china collection or paint some mismatching chairs for your refectory dining table.

Shaping Your Space

Make your spaces fun and functional by following the basic rules of good layout, then add in personal touches to bring a room to life

'Make a furniture plan – this is a simple step that most people think they don't need. The pros all do it for their clients.' *Tom Delavan, designer*

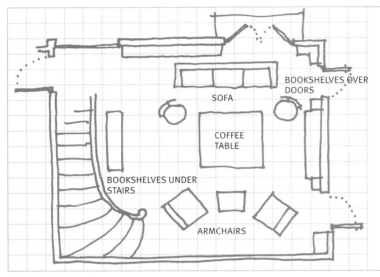

BOOKSHELVES OVER DOORS

SOFA

COFFEE TABLE

BOOKSHELVES UNDER STAIRS

ARMCHAIRS

LIVING ROOM PLAN

- In larger spaces make a separate quiet space for reading.
- Plan to have some storage, either built-in or freestanding.
- Create a cosy welcoming space by placing furniture around a focal point such as a generous-sized coffee table.
- Rugs anchor a room, providing definition for seating areas.
- Use furniture such as console tables to define and divide different areas of activity.
- Always aim to include a sofa plus at least two other seats to provide flexibility.
- If you need to work with specific architectural features, statement furniture or a collection of books, art or other objects, let them dictate the way you approach your home.

BLACK AND WHITE AND READ *Opposite below left* In his Paris apartment, Frédéric Méchiche designed the living room around his vast book collection. The traditional architecture makes a pleasing counterpoint to the modern furniture ranged round the room.

BOOKS DO MAKE A SPACE *Opposite below right* Integral bookshelves meld into the original architecture and create an inviting environment for a collection of mid-century and contemporary leather seating.

DISGUISED ELEGANCE *Below left* Tine Kjeldsen of Tine K Home in Denmark created kitchen units that appear to be more like furniture, which is a great way to furnish a kitchen/living/dining space.

VERSATILE SPACE *Below right* Elsewhere in the kitchen/diner a small rustic table doubles up as a food preparation space or a temporary workstation. Freestanding storage positioned near by means kitchen tableware is always close at hand.

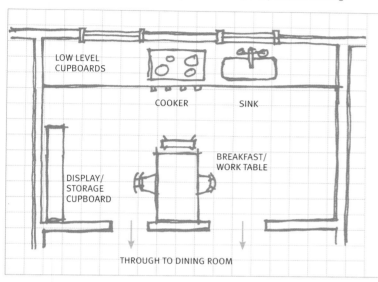

LOW LEVEL CUPBOARDS

COOKER   SINK

DISPLAY/ STORAGE CUPBOARD

BREAKFAST/ WORK TABLE

THROUGH TO DINING ROOM

KITCHEN PLAN

- Place sink, fridge and cooker in a loose triangle to make efficient use of the space.
- Good layouts that work for kitchens are U-shaped, L-shaped and island formations.
- In small rooms, use built-in furniture to maximize storage space.
- In larger spaces incorporate an eating area or a multi-functional island.
- Try using open shelving instead of matchy-matchy wall cupboards and display your favourite china collection.
- Functional floors are essential – opt for materials that are waterproof, durable and easy to clean such as tiles, linoleum or vinyl.

HIDDEN STORAGE *Below left* A walk-in closet is hidden behind a run of semi-opaque curtains that are suspended behind a reclaimed wooden bed in Marc and Melissa Palazzo's Orange County home.

FAUX WALL *Below right* To give the illusion of a wall, a large painting is suspended on wire from the inobtrusive curtain rail attached to the ceiling. The bed has no headboard, which adds to the illusion.

'When I'm working on a room I think of textures, colours and prints that would make me feel warm and inspired.

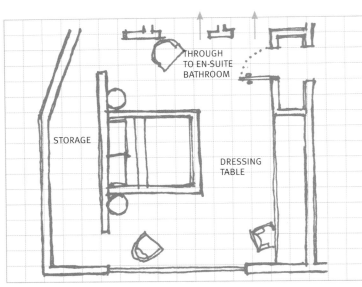

STORAGE

THROUGH TO EN-SUITE BATHROOM

DRESSING TABLE

BEDROOM PLAN

- Make the most of your bed since it's the obvious focal point in your sleeping space.
- Good reading lights and bedside tables are a must.
- Edit your clothes and shoes to fit your available space and consider building in more storage if you don't have enough.
- Think about dividing off areas for clothes storage with curtains, screens or half-height walls too.
- Make built-in cupboards more interesting by inserting wallpaper panelling, mirrors or decorative handles.
- Display favourite sketches and drawings from favourite places on the walls.
- Consider using the area under the bed for additional storage.

SEEING DOUBLE *Below left* In a shared bathroom a generous double trough-style sink is perfectly at home beneath a wall mirror placed horizontally to become a generous vanity mirror.

PRIVATE SPACE *Below right* The Palazzos created a false wall and opening so that a walk-in shower and WC could be tucked behind the main bathroom, with its freestanding bath and spacious double sink.

For example, my bedroom is minimal, because I want to feel at peace.' *Amy Butler, designer*

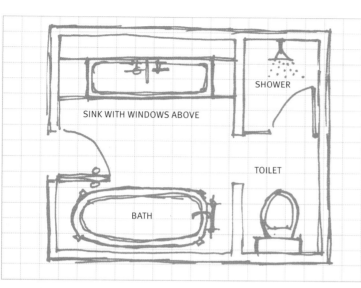

SHOWER

SINK WITH WINDOWS ABOVE

TOILET

BATH

BATHROOM PLAN

- Do you need a bath in your bathroom or do you only take showers? Can you squeeze in an en-suite?
- Bathrooms always need storage, so consider wall cupboards or built-in units.
- Sometimes two sinks are better than one. Make a feature of a pair by fitting interesting taps or sourcing unusual mirrors for each one.
- Use tiling as a decorative feature. Metro tiles will give a simple retro feel, while colourful mosaic or mismatching floral tiles echo the Mediterranean or eccentric country style.
- Bold, graphic wallpaper can enliven bathroom spaces.
- Keep floors practical and easy to keep clean. Use ceramic tiles, polished concrete or vinyl coverings.

Architectural Considerations

Make the most of your structural assets

ECLECTIC COMFORT *Below* In Amy Butler's home she has combined one-off mid-century pieces with stylish ethnic accessories in a living space that has additional ceiling windows to maximize the light.

INDUSTRIAL SPACE *Opposite* Converted buildings often look best painted white so the architecture itself can take centre stage. A swing has been hung from the rafters to accentuate the height of the space.

Highlight architectural mouldings by painting them a defining colour or the same colour as the ceiling when you use a different wall colour.

In a traditional space add contemporary furniture to provide a pleasing old with new counterpoint.

Draw attention to a focal point such as a fireplace or wall panelling by leaving the space around it free from furniture or pictures.

Where windows are generous, keep the dressing to a minimum so you can emphasize their shape and make them a big part of the space.

WORKING WITH THE BUILDING

Play with scale in a room that has high ceilings. Introduce oversized elements such as overhead lights, huge plants or generous sofas to emphasize the space and make a statement.

Think about flooring. Whether it is stripped wood, gloss-painted concrete or ceramic tiles, consider keeping it plain so that the space itself grabs all the attention.

Where skirting boards are deep and generous, consider painting them the same colour as the other architectural features such as mouldings, picture rails and dados.

'Clean lines in a well-
designed background
are the beginning to any
successful job. I believe
modern architecture is the
perfect canvas to bring in
any time period you want
to work with, but with any
space one should utilize
the architecture to show
off the furnishings to their
best advantage.'

Vicente Wolf, designer

USING YOUR SPACE

Using your space well means making the most of your existing building and decorating it in keeping with the core components of walls, floors and ceilings. If you have high ceilings, for instance, you immediately have more options for maximizing your space with a mezzanine or tall bespoke walls of storage. If you have a series of small rooms you may want to open them out by knocking down a wall or making a half-height room divider to create different areas in a single room, while improving the natural light.

Amy Neunsinger's industrial-style 1950s home in the Laurel Canyon area of Los Angeles has been massively extended in keeping with the original framework and includes hard edges such as concrete floors, exposed ceiling beams, bare metal-framed windows and exposed air ducts.

ONE-SPACE LIVING The open plan living and dining space capitalizes on large windows and a light-filled, high-ceilinged space. A statement chandelier, a painted and aged dining table mixed with steel dining chairs and a careworn wall are an interesting combination, while the entire ground floor has a dark painted floor to unify the space.

'At night it feels so cavernous and cosy, when you've got candles lit and they pick up the texture of the wall. During the day, it is different completely. It can be everything from austere to decadent.'

Amy Neunsinger

'I think of the whole house as South of France meets industrial. I just love pure function. But then there's the softer, female stuff that's important to me too.' *Amy Neunsinger*

Amy employed architect Juan-Felipe Goldstein to oversee the reconfiguring of the space from a modest 1950s house to a spacious and welcoming family home. The overall impression here though is one of cool comfort. Many of the walls have been left untreated, with their natural brick and concrete patina providing a unique warmth and texture. During the renovation Goldstein called up Amy and put in a plea that the walls were so attractive in their pared back state that she should consider leaving them as they were, which she did. They inspired the overall decoration of the house and texture is now key throughout the extended home. You can see it on zinc tables, in painted rattan, on animal-skin rugs and comfortable cotton slipcovers. Mixing all these different materials together creates a cohesive and surprising warmth given the lack of soft surfaces in the space.

INDUSTRIAL CHIC In a hard-edged space remember to soften the edges. Here a giant photographic print on canvas adds a natural seascape to an otherwise pure white wall and a squashy, comfortable sofa plus African carved-wood tables from a Santa Monica flea market look inviting against the glossy grey concrete floor.

ALFRED STIEGLITZ

LIGHT AND BRIGHT *Left* White upholstery always looks great in bright white-on-white spaces, where there are traces of dark colours and woods to create contrasts. Here an ethnic wooden console stops the seating area from becoming lost in whiteness and a fabulous chunky metal coffee table sits on animal-skin rugs.

The family room has plump, squishy sofas and two large round occasional tables with an ethnic vibe for a relaxed atmosphere.

An island layout in the kitchen gives maximum flexibility and frees up wall space for large French windows.

STAIRS TO FIRST FLOOR

FAMILY/ MEDIA ROOM

KITCHEN/ DINING ROOM

GARDEN ROOM

LIVING ROOM

A garden room brings the outdoors in so that even on rainy days you can still enjoy natural surroundings.

In the living room white walls and furniture match in with the white ceiling rafters for a cool and airy but welcoming space.

COOK'S KITCHEN *Left* Custom-made units slip effortlessly into the industrial space where utility meets chic in the form of sleek stainless steel appliances and open shelving, warmed up with vintage accessories.

Letting in the Light

It's free, it's natural – use it wisely

There is nothing more appealing than a comfortable room bathed in natural light that changes through the day. It's always worth checking the orientation of a room in relation to the sun to work out whether you are likely have a light-filled space in the morning, evening or – the best of all – for the whole day. Knowing which direction the light is coming from will help you decide what colours to use in the room to enhance or dampen the light.

WALL LIGHT In designer Vicente Wolf's New York apartment a wall of sliding glass doors and natural light provide an enticing glimpse of books, paintings and decorative objects on the other side.

LIGHT MATTERS

North-facing rooms in the northern hemisphere have a natural grey quality to them that can be made to look more dingy if bathed in brilliant white paint. Choose cool greys to warm up spaces such as these.

Jewel-bright sunlit rooms can stand big bold shades of fuchsia or topaz so go with the colourful vibe if light is not an issue.

If you are not overlooked, leave windows bare where light is sparse to maximize the flow of rays into the room.

Consider installing a rooflight to bring in additional daylight in a dark space.

Install an internal window, glass bricks or frosted glass panels between rooms to steal light from another space that may have access to light coming in from the outside.

Use sheer roller blinds of muslin or linen where some privacy is required but you need to encourage the light, too, during the day.

Opt for pale colours in light-starved spaces and stick to the neutral end of the spectrum for the best effect.

PALE AND NEUTRAL
Opposite top Anita Kaushal's London living room is painted a delicate pale grey. This colour always makes the most of cold northern light and warms a space in European climes.

OVERHEAD PROJECTION *This page* A rooflight combines with French windows to maximize natural light in this kitchen/diner, while a pale wooden floor and walls contribute to the airy atmosphere. Even the marble tabletop reflects natural light upwards.

'There's a visceral connection between our surroundings and our mood, and the amount and quality of light is the first element that dictates those moods.'

Marcia Zia-Priven, lighting designer

'In the living room we found that the niche formed a natural space for our heirloom sofa and the art above it. It makes a good focal point when looking towards the living room.'

Claus Robenhagen

SOFT MODERN Dark wooden floors always help to anchor a space. Here they link a series of rooms as well as providing accent colour in a living room, together with a retro lamp, black and white prints and cushion detailing.

CASE STUDY

LINKING SPACES

The method of placing rooms in a single line, with doors placed at the same point in each room to provide a vista from one end to the other was first used in grand houses such as the Versailles Palace in Paris but the same arrangement is often found in city apartments and in cottages. Decorating a series of interlinking spaces is a fun challenge; you always have to check the view out of a room into the next one works with the room you are in.

The Copenhagen apartment of fashion designer Heidi Hofmann Møller and gallery director Claus Robenhagen is a charming space made to feel more spacious by this type of enfilade arrangement.

ENFILADE SPACES A unique view from the bedroom, through the dining space and out to the study and the living room means there can be no style secrets. The furniture of each room has to work with each adjacent space.

It is an arrangement most commonly seen in public spaces, such as art galleries and museums, which is apt since Claus is himself involved in an art gallery. 'We really enjoy how the four rooms connect together in the apartment. It almost feels like one room, yet each space is also well defined, which gives it a certain flexibility.'

The dining room is at the centre of the apartment and this is often used as an entertaining space. 'The entryway is very small so this has become a convenient stop en-route to the other rooms. When we entertain,' says Heidi, 'dinners or parties tend to start with drinks in the middle room – and then end with more drinks and sometimes dancing in the same space.' The double doors were designed to emphasize the linear layout. On one side is the private space of the bedroom, where words such as 'heirloom' and 'gifted' are printed on the surface, while the dining room side is inspired by the 1980s Italian Memphis Style aesthetic that they both really enjoy.

On moving in four years ago, the couple, who had fallen in love with the light, spacious feel of the apartment, set about renovating the space completely, removing old layers of wallpaper, painting the floors, renewing the electrics and recarving the architectural mouldings, which were disguised by so many layers of paint it was hard to see what they should look like. Both the kitchen and the bathroom were replaced.

They decided to paint the floors black by applying a water-based paint, then sealing it with a coat of water-based lacquer on top. It was easy to work with and is really quite durable. 'We like the black colour as it gives focus to the space and makes the colours of the rest of the room stand out.'

'The bespoke double doors that lead from the dining room to the bedroom were designed by Bank/Rau, two artists that work together. The inspiration comes from the fact that the doors bind together some of the most central rooms in the apartment.'

Heidi Hofmann Møller

'Our personal style can best be summed up as a mix of different decades, with an end result that is colourful, personal and innovative.'

Claus Robenhagen

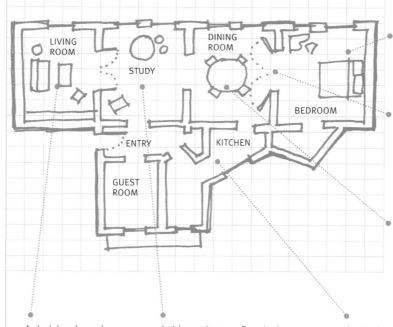

DESERT ISLAND ART *Above left*
A wirework image of a scrolled map is a neat wall decoration against a contemporary bentwood easy chair in the study area in between the living room and the dining room.

STATEMENT DINING *Above right*
At the centre of the apartment, an Eero Saarinen Tulip table is pride of place, its oval shape providing a smooth organic form amongst a series of square and rectangular spaces.

CUSHION HEADBOARD *Opposite*
Plumped cushions ranged across the top of the bed replace a conventional headboard and provide touches of colour in the bedroom.

The main rooms of the apartment are arranged *enfilade*, with one room leading to the next.

Double doors between the dining space and the bedroom were custom-made to provide a statement piece of design in the apartment.

An oval marble Tulip table is placed in the centre of the room and forms a focal point from both the bedroom and the work room.

A dark hardwood floor runs through the apartment, unifying the space and making it feel larger.

A tidy work room fits nicely between the living room and dining room and also serves as a drop off spot for keys and bags as it is directly off the entry hall.

The kitchen fits neatly into a cosy space with a charming balcony with a table for two facing the rear courtyard of the building.

Dividing Space

*Create new shapes and functions
by clever division of your basic rooms*

Creative ways of dividing space may range from architectural solutions, where faux walls act as space definers or define a change of function, to one-off decorative pieces that demarcate an area, such as a retro folding screen or a large piece of traditional furniture. Whatever method you choose, room dividers are a versatile way of organizing your space to make it work harder.

GLAZED DOORS *Below* In Nathalie Leté's Parisian apartment, glazed metal-framed doors frame a bright and whimsical feminine bedroom. By day they open out to extend the living area, but by night floor-to-ceiling curtains are drawn to enclose the bedroom and create a semi-tented feel, Bedouin-style.

PLAY DAYS *Opposite* This functional, modern house in Denmark incorporates half-height walls to divide the space into a child's play area that is separate but easily accessible from the adult work and dining areas.

WORKING WITH WHAT YOU HAVE

Make room dividers really work hard by incorporating storage into them in the form of shelves or cupboards.

Sliding doors or screens can be made from wood or frosted glass panels or can be decorated with a mural.

Half-height room dividers work as subtle screens when dividing off a particular zone, such as a freestanding bath in a bedroom, a work area in a living space or a seating area in a kitchen.

Freestanding furniture can become a good room-dividing solution: try a unit of openplan pigeon holes on castors that doubles up as a storage and display place.

Folding screens vary from Japanese-style grids of wood and rice paper, fabric-covered concertinas or vintage hospital screens made from scaffolding-type poles and covered with muslin or other lightweight fabric.

Create an open recess in which to place a discreet shower room, a small dressing area or a compact work space.

Use a room divider as a dual-purpose functional space: bathroom on one side, shower on the other; shelves for storage on display on one side and utility room storage on the other; bed on one side, bathroom on the other.

Greenery in the form of large fig trees or other large household plants in striking containers are good for defining different zones in a living room.

'My clients place high priority on spaces that have multiple functions, such as family room and dining space, living room and TV space, sunroom and breakfast room plus comfortable, great-looking sectional sofas.'

Betsy Burnham, designer

OLD WITH NEW By mixing vintage furniture such as painted cupboards with modern-day classics such as Eames dining chairs, Anna-Malin disguises the fact that her house is a contemporary space.

'Where I grew up, there are mountains and lots of snow so that is why I use white as a foundation colour in my home. It's flexible and versatile.' *Anna-Malin Lindgren*

KITCHEN CHIC The room exudes comfort and effortless style, drawing your eye to the clever combinations of furniture and materials, as well as the softening of clean architectural lines with the addition of curvy painted rattan chairs and tables.

FLEXIBLE SPACES

Flexible spaces make sense for homes in which there are growing families. Dividing up a large space into different activity zones is one way of preserving flexibility. A living space may be divided by a temporary room divider, to allow a change of use at a later date.

Anna-Malin Lindgren's home in Helsingborg, Sweden is a truly flexible space. Before moving in Anna-Malin spent some time making design decisions about the use of each room and how the space should flow. She and husband Anders selected materials such as flooring, kitchen units and wall colours. Natural light was an issue for them so they decided to add transom windows over the internal doors and in the ceiling upstairs to let in more light.

From northern Sweden originally, Anna-Malin likes to connect with things in a spiritual way rather than simply choosing off-the-peg solutions when it comes to furniture or fittings. The reindeer furs in the living room are cruelty-free in that they are harvested for meat and the furs are also used so nothing is wasted.

Although Anna-Malin would prefer to live in an older house – this one is only a few years old – she has managed to create a sense of timeless comfort. 'I've learnt to work with the home and not against it, making it reflect my taste and style and adapting the space to fit in with our lifestyle that incorporates two young children and plenty of comings and goings, both of people and activities.'

SCREEN MAGIC *Above* A black-painted wall divides the living/dining space from the kitchen area. In the centre is a discreetly mounted flatscreen TV, with home entertainment accessories stored beneath in a contemporary low-level cabinet.

WARM COMFORT *Opposite above* Squashy period sofas and generously filled cushions in different shapes and sizes, covered in a variety of fabrics and textures provide ease. Clustered around a painted coffee table, the furniture creates an intimate conversation and relaxing area.

MODERN TRADITION *Opposite below* Throughout the house pieces of vintage and period furniture soften the clean architectural lines. Black and white are key base colours for the decorating scheme.

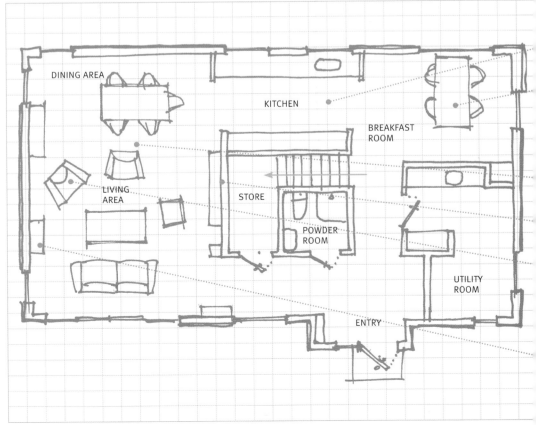

'I like a cold and warm contrast in my home created with materials and colours. The reindeer furs in the living room warm up the white space.' *Anna-Malin Lindgren*

A change of flooring in the kitchen space provides definition for a room without walls.

A dining table in the kitchen area doubles up as a craft space or a work area during the day. An extendable dining table means it can be moved around the space according to needs.

The living and dining space is a flexible area that can over time become a live/work space or a live/play space as small children get bigger.

The wall that divides the living space and the kitchen/diner and stairwell is painted black so as to disguise the flatscreen TV.

Ultra comfortable chairs and a sofa provide a touch of period charm in an otherwise contemporary space. Soft pale plum and mulberry tones on the furniture warm up the white space.

Freestanding storage and display units are flexible and can be moved around the space when required.

Floors & Walls

Careful thinking about these vital surfaces can set the tone for how you want your space to feel

Far from being the 'boring bits', walls and floors can absolutely make a space, so getting these surfaces right is an important task. Whether you choose wooden floors and rugs or carpeting, painted walls or wallpaper, your choices will often influence what style of decorating works best for the rest of the room.

'I love using chalkboard paint – it's the perfect black-but-not-pure-black and has a great matt finish. I've used it on walls, furniture, lamp bases and vases.'

Belinda Graham, blogger

Decorating with Walls Your walls offer plenty of choices when it comes to decorating. From matt or glossy paint finishes, to bold floral, geometric or patterned wallpaper and even fabric, you can apply your chosen finish to just one wall or bathe a whole room in your favourite wallpaper or paint colour. Panelled walls or tongue-and-groove dado-height panels merit carefully chosen colours, either muted or bold depending on what you love.

CLASSIC GREY *Above left* Painting walls grey is like dressing in black and white. It is versatile and always stylish, allowing you to embellish the overall effect with small dashes of other colours.

BLACKBOARD WALLS *Above right* In a kitchen or children's play room use blackboard paint on walls and doors to create a permanent space for drawing, doodling and list-making.

Wooden Floors If you have a busy family home, an urban loft or a traditional country cottage, wooden floors will work in all of these spaces. Stripped floors are great in older houses, while bleached or painted glossy boards look ultra smart in modern or retro industrial spaces. They are also easy to maintain and keep clean.

Softening Wooden Floors Rugs and runners work really well with wooden floors and will also add colour and pattern to a neutrally decorated room. Rectangular, square or circular shapes anchor or define specific areas in a living room, while runners work well in hallways and bathrooms. If you don't like the thought of hard floors in bedrooms or children's rooms, then carpeting is a relatively affordable option.

FLOOR & WALL DECISIONS

In an old or a new building leaving bricks exposed or painting them are both options. Old redbrick, especially round a fireplace, is warming, while white-painted bricks are a contemporary solution.

Wood is versatile and hardwearing in areas of heavy use such as hallways and living rooms.

Cosy up a space with rugs and ring the changes with one for summer and one for winter.

Panelled walls never fail to make a room feel welcoming. Paint them a similar colour to the walls for a unifying effect or a distinct colour to place a visual emphasis on them.

Wallpaper is available in so many designs it is capable of altering the style of a room.

Painted floors work well in small or large spaces.

CURVED AIR *Left* Bleached floorboards and generous windows give this living room an airy feel. On a diagonal wall a large pigeon-hole bookcase is both functional and decorative.

'Be bold and paint a feature wall, table, and floor. Don't worry, it's like a hair cut, therefore not permanent.'

Carrie McCarthy, author

'Most rooms need a rug – a room without a rug can appear unwelcoming and unfinished. It brings a sense of luxury to a room; the colour, pattern and texture lend a feeling of comfort and personality.'

Suzanne Sharp, The Rug Company

UNDERSTATED GLAMOUR *Below* In a room where the furniture takes centre stage and the floor is cool concrete, discreet animal skin rugs placed in the seating area make a wonderful counterpoint to both the furniture and the intricate chandelier. They define the space but also lend a neat touch of warmth and sophistication.

DARK DEFINITION *Opposite* In cool spaces anchor the pale seas of white with a glossy dark wooden floor. It will provide sharp definition in a room and allow furniture, textures and artworks to come to the foreground.

'I see white environments as an opportunity to draw attention to elements that might otherwise be lost in a more colourful setting. The neutrality of white allows texture, shadow and light to become focal points rather than afterthoughts.'

Anna Dorfman, graphic designer/ blogger

Rugs

In spaces with hard wooden or concrete floors, rugs are the vital ingredient for providing decoration, comfort and texture

FUCHSIA PERFECT *Below* In Alayne Patrick's Brooklyn apartment she has brought an Asian textiles vibe to the space and punctuated it with a striped cotton dhurrie in bleached raspberry and pale sky blue.

NATIONAL PRIDE *Opposite* Jonathan Adler and Simon Doonan's eclectic office space nods in the direction of Simon's nationality with a Union Jack rug in navy and lime in a statement that is both stylish and quirky.

CHOOSING RUGS

Choose a shape that complements your space. Circular rugs work well in square living rooms. Runners are good for hallways and landings or other narrow spaces.

Rugs make good alternatives to carpets, especially in areas of heavy use such as living rooms and children's rooms.

Look at many types and styles of rugs before you make your final decision. Rug shops will usually lend you a few styles so you can view them in situ before making a final choice.

From traditional Indian dhurries and Oriental rugs to woven wool and animal skins, rugs are not merely finishing touches in rooms. They often provide both a focal point and a sense of welcome, especially in living rooms and hallways. Rugs perform the dual task of protecting hard flooring and adding comfort to a space. Pattern and texture are just as important as materials when it comes to rug design, so consider all these when you are thinking about a centrepiece for a room.

Scandinavian woven cotton runners look great on bleached or dark wooden floors. Chunky seagrass matting and sheepskin rugs also work well on wood, while rag rugs and thick woven wool always provide comfort and colour. On concrete, animal skins provide a definite warmth.

'Beautifully patterned rugs always wake a space up.'

Lulu deKwiatkowski, designer

'Don't skimp on rugs. I prefer big rugs that really surround as well as define a living room.'

Maxwell Gillingham-Ryan, interior designer/blogger

COMPACT SPACE

Living in small spaces calls for a sense of order and a smart but cosy approach to decorating. There is no room for clutter so be ruthless in editing your belongings and living with only what you need. Use every inch of space – build shelving into generous cupboard spaces or see whether a fold-down desk or additional storage can be incorporated.

This compact space in Manhattan is decorated to give an instant sense of comfort and interest. All the elements flow together smoothly and with so much to feast the eye on, the small scale is pushed to the background. Style writer and interior designer Rita Konig has bestowed her British sense of comfort on her tiny apartment.

ROOM WITH A VIEW
Compact spaces need to be tidy at all times as all the rooms are often on show. This pretty bedroom is snug and inviting seen from the living room where the floral wallpaper and scalloped edges of headboard and bedding become soft and appealing focal points.

'Start with thinking about how you live, then plan a layout of rooms and furniture to suit your lifestyle before you get on to the details about what style to follow.'

Rita Konig

CALM COMFORT
Soothing grey walls, a very personal collection of pictures and large sofa in a small living area create a cosy ambience that disguises the compact overall space.

'The best rooms in a home are always comfortable, tranquil and have a strong sense of the person that lives there. Rooms should be a culmination of things and it is hard to create that in an instant,' says Rita. 'I've moved several times in New York so when I moved to this space I decided to reupholster some key pieces of furniture to ring the changes.' This is a good way of updating the look of a room for not too much outlay.

'My pictures are really important to me and I had quite a few of them brought over from London,' explains Rita. 'The best interior designer can decorate your home, but without pictures on the walls it will lack a dimension that I find so important.

'One of my favourite colours is a pale grey from the Paint Library in London. It is always bright and clean and is a great foil for many other colours. I often combine it with pink and green to create a very soothing and warming scheme. I like storage and order to form part of the decorating, which is why I like the drinks tray, book shelves, linen closet and pantry that have become a part of the space itself in my apartment. I've also adapted a closet to become a mini office.'

WALK-THROUGH KITCHEN *Left* Neatly tucked into a hallway, Rita Konig's kitchen combines a wall-mounted bookshelf for cookery books and a galley-style practical food preparation area.

PICTURE PERFECT *Opposite* Cosy and colourful seating, a drinks table and interesting art on the walls combine to create the perfect welcome. Use bright velvet upholstery as a counterpoint to pale walls.

At one end of the apartment the bedroom opens on to the living room so is decorated to be 'on show' when required.

A sofa is used along with three occasional chairs to create cosy seating areas in a living space that is at the heart of the apartment.

Off the central living room a small closet has been used to house a mini office with the addition of new shelving.

A large entryway has been converted into a welcoming walk-through kitchen space.

LOVE

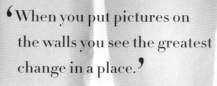

'When you put pictures on the walls you see the greatest change in a place.'

Rita Konig

Increasing Space

Ingenious use of space can yield dividends in small spaces

Compact living calls for neat ideas as well as tidy spaces. There are various ways of increasing your living space while not eating up valuable parts of the original floor area. You can quite often shoehorn additional living, working or sleeping spaces into tiny areas such as cupboards, enclosed upper level capsules or by adding a mezzanine level to tall spaces.

Split-level spaces are one way of including different zones in a living space. Mezzanines are good for creating libraries or reading areas above living spaces, which additional sleeping spaces can appear above kitchens, off first floor landings or incorporated into existing bedrooms. Where a lot of living has been layered into spaces of awkward shapes and varying heights, getting from one area to another may call for a variety of different ladders, shallow permanent steps or temporary stairs. While ladders are versatile and useful in split-level lofts and apartments, safety is a key consideration. Small children, toddlers and even teenagers are often drawn to stairs and cannot resist exploring them. If you do not want to be forever checking up on them, think about whether a small, discreet staircase in steel or wood may be a better solution.

CAPSULE BEDROOM *Above* In Lyndsay Caleo and Fitzhugh Karol's Brooklyn home, their one-space living area has room for a capsule sleeping area tucked above the kitchen space. Curtained off when not in use, it is reached via a vintage ladder when required.

'Draw a floor plan to scale and experiment with furniture placement. Fill wall recesses with shelves and remember that wall-mounted cabinets free up floor space.'

Deborah Bibby, editor in chief

MAKING SPACE

Look at your home as a 3D shell so you can assess where and how to increase your space. A tall hallway could incorporate a sleeping capsule or a bedroom could double up as a creative space by adding a mezzanine level.

Landings are good places for slotting in a mini home office or a day bed for younger overnight guests. In tall bedrooms, consider building a high bunk and creating a workstation beneath it.

Consider dividing rooms to provide separate spaces for different activities.

If space is tight, think about using transparent walls or windows to divide the different zones but preserve a sense of space.

'My husband and I like our home to be very uncluttered, so built-in storage gives the house a more calming, tranquil quality. We invested a lot in hidden storage so we don't have to look at all our stuff all the time.' *Jessie Randall, designer*

DAY BEDS AND DADOS *Above* In a large light-filled space a mezzanine landing has been designed to become a daytime relaxation area, benefiting from fabulous natural daylight and open views across the living spaces, in the home of Pal + Smith designers Marc and Melissa Palazzo.

SMALL AND SMART In a compact New York apartment Liz Bauer has managed to cleverly create a series of rooms without compromising on style or a sense of space. Instead, it feels like a classic home because she has managed to shoehorn a foyer, dining room, living room, dressing room, bedroom, kitchen and bathroom into what is essentially one studio space.

'Use what you have and add to it. Colour is important, and I cannot live without pattern.'

Liz Bauer

ONE ROOM LIVING

Living in one space calls for an exacting use of the floor area. Every single piece of furniture has to be fit for purpose and be as versatile as possible. An occasional table needs to include storage, a bed will need to have hidden clothes boxes beneath it and the floor space should be kept uncluttered to encourage natural light to flow through the space.

This one-room apartment belonging to New York interior designer Liz Bauer has been transformed using modern twists, traditional elements and a feminine touch into a smart but inviting space whose limited floor area is well disguised by clever design techniques. Bauer initially installed a faux fireplace as the first focal point in the living room, then a transparent vintage screen was used to demarcate the bedroom from the living space, together with bold wallpaper on the ceiling and walls around the bed. The eye is naturally drawn to the patterned walls rather than the fact there is a bed at the end of the living space. 'I turned the small hallway into a dressing room. It seemed like such dead space to me, and living in NYC and having dead space is not an option! It houses a closet and is right next to the bathroom, so it just seemed like the logical place for me to get dressed and put on make-up,' says Bauer.

TRADITIONAL LIVING By mixing interesting art, colourful textiles and upholstery from Designers Guild and Manuel Canovas plus vibrant table lamps along one wall, then complementing them with a transparent drinks trolley and coffee table, Bauer manages to bring the living space to life while disguising its limited size.

'Architectural details are a must for me as I grew up in a very traditional home. Although the space is technically a studio, I immediately knew that I could define the space into different areas and give more of a classic home feel.' *Liz Bauer*

STORAGE AND DISPLAY *Right* Liz takes a practical approach to space: 'Although I have made my apartment deliberately functional, I do not have room to display everything. At some point, in another home, I am sure the white cabinet will once again house china and crystal. For now, it is functional storage.'

The entryway is used for storage and display as you enter the apartment.

A small hallway connecting the bathroom to the main living space was converted into a dressing area outside the bathroom.

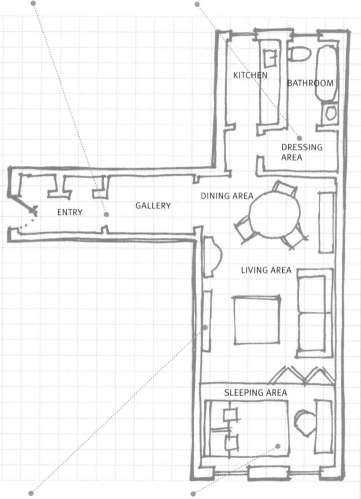

KITCHEN

BATHROOM

DRESSING AREA

DINING AREA

ENTRY

GALLERY

LIVING AREA

SLEEPING AREA

A faux fireplace has been added to provide a focal point opposite the sofa.

Divided off with a transparent vintage glass screen, the bed is placed across the space so that the natural light can flow in freely.

DESIGNING WITH WALLPAPER *Right* Papering the walls and ceiling at the end of the living space creates a mini sleeping haven. Bauer used a welcoming blue and white paper from Rose Cummings punctuated with rose pink lampshades and art.

Colour Tricks

Colour is one of the most powerful of decorators' tools. Relatively economical to use, fun to choose but also easy to get wrong, so some experimentation is a good idea

'Wallpaper or paint the interiors of your bookshelves and, if you can afford to, the ceiling or an accent wall.' *Celerie Kemble, designer*

MODERN DISPLAY *Above* Painting the space behind display shelves a vivid colour provides a visual focus and a backdrop for your collection, whether it is china or other decorative objects.

DARK CHOCOLATE *Opposite* Combining a range of tones in one colourway makes a sophisticated statement. Minky, mole-like browns and soft cappuccinos on a range of fabrics and textures in a bedroom presents an enticing picture.

COLOUR MAGIC

For instant impact paint one wall in a living room or bedroom in a bold, vivid colour. Choose the wall that will make the most dramatic statement.

In a large room where you want to enhance a sense of enclosure and seclusion, opposing walls can be painted the same colour.

You can add highly patterned wallpaper to one wall to create a feature in a room where there is no natural focal point.

In a room dominated by neutral colours add in vivid contrast colour as accents on upholstery, cushions or artwork. Strong tones such as orange, citrus lime or red work well as vivid jolts of colour in this way.

Infusing a room with bold colour is one of the best decorating tools to create an instant mood or a certain style. Think warm blues, hot pinks or sunshine yellows. They will all create a cosy space in a small room and detract from the room's natural dimensions.

Remember that red will always warm and enclose while white will always expand and lighten a space. When choosing paint colours, always opt for a shade or two lighter than what you are naturally drawn to. Paint chips often deceive.

Steer away from brilliant white paint. It contains a blue caste that will make northern rooms dull and grey. Instead, opt for a standard white that includes a hint of pink pigment for maximum 'whiteness' on the finished wall.

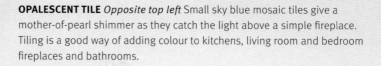

CITRUS DEFINITION *This page* Inject some colour by painting around artworks or using cushions or rugs to make a colour statement. Flowers are also a good means of shifting the colour direction one way or another in a living room or bedroom.

OPALESCENT TILE *Opposite top left* Small sky blue mosaic tiles give a mother-of-pearl shimmer as they catch the light above a simple fireplace. Tiling is a good way of adding colour to kitchens, living room and bedroom fireplaces and bathrooms.

BANDS OF COLOUR *Opposite top right* Apply bold colours midway up a wall to lessen their impact but provide a visual feast when moving from one room to another. Use paint or wallpaper to create the colour and add in complementary tones for punctuation.

PASTEL PRIMARIES *Opposite bottom left* Soft shades of blue, red and green used as accents in all-white kitchens are fresh and inviting. Experiment with lighter or darker tones of the colours you are naturally drawn towards to create a variety of palettes.

RASPBERRY PINK *Opposite bottom right* Pale pink linen walls in Christine d'Ornano's London home are subtle but hugely warming. Some colours will change character according to how they are used. A gloss grey will be colder than a chalky paint, while blue can bear to be shiny as well as matt.

'Colour creates life and energy. It can be uplifting and make us smile and your home should make you smile, you should be happy there. What better way to achieve this than by infusing beautiful colour into your space . . .' *Shannon Fricke, stylist*

"We all have our own STYLE and personality to our work, even if we follow the same step-by-step instructions."

Lotta Jansdotter

Setting Your Style

'I love a well-travelled, eclectic house with furniture and objects, layered one upon the other, that tell a story about who lives there, where they've been and what they love. There's nothing worse than walking into someone's house that looks like they just called up a decorator!' *Eddie Ross, designer*

ELEGANT LIVING *This page* Deciding on a personal style is so often about living with what you love, whether it is a collection of paintings, favourite furniture styles, colours that inspire you or objects that hold a special significance. Run with your instinct and you won't often go wrong.

DESIGN CLASSIC *Previous page* Setting your style may be a matter of selecting a certain piece of furniture and allowing it to lead the way elsewhere in the room. Here an Ercol sofa forms the basis of a mid-century aesthetic.

FEELING THE STYLE

Once you move away from home into your first property you learn a simple truth: this is the one place where you can truly express yourself and let your imagination run wild. Discovering your style sensibility and why you are attracted to certain things is one of the most joyful and emotionally freeing processes of decorating. Once you grasp that your home is your space to experiment with new ideas it's smart to explore a little and learn about what you truly connect with, and why, so you can shop smarter, faster, have less return purchases and truly love the space you're living in. When your home authentically reflects those living there, which is the ultimate goal, you can enjoy domestic life even more – making your bed is more interesting when you've learned how to layer pattern, and simply walking into your home at the end of a long day gives you a warm, welcoming feeling.

HAVE YOU EVER wondered why you are always drawn to painted furniture or mid-century modern ceramics? Why you can't walk past a flea market without stopping for just a peek? Why you linger over a design blog or a magazine that hones in on feminine finds or classic furniture? This is where you need to pull out a small notebook and start taking note of what interests you and why.

Quick kitchen renovation Your ideas can be composed in a large journal and need not always be focused on a complete room design. In this example, a kitchen that needs a few modern updates is in the works. Bright textiles, mismatched dishware, bold ceramic pitchers, fresh flowers and vibrant floral wallpaper set the tone for a quick renovation.

'Saturate yourself with visual reference. Magazines, books, websites, art galleries, museums, shops. You can't know what styles you like if you don't have knowledge of what's out there.' *Atlanta Bartlett, designer*

HAPPINESS IS . . .
This craft room is a creative workshop for Californian stylist and photographer Leslie Shewring. She has surrounded herself with brightly coloured objects against a white background so that this room sparks her creativity and simply brings her joy.

Before you start collecting and analyzing your inspirations, first let's stomp out a common misconception. Some people think there is too much choice and visual overload and encourage taking time out or logging off in order to feel more inspired. While this is true from time to time, exploration is really the key to tapping into your likes and dislikes. We are lucky to have such a broad choice laid out before us. Shopping for interiors has become as much fun as shopping for clothes with the range of stylish finds out there. With retail outlets, boutiques, online shops, sample sales, pop-up shops, catalogues, home shopping television shows and other great resources, home decorating has certainly evolved for the better and choices are no longer as limited as they were in past generations. If you sometimes feel overwhelmed by choice and have a hard time defining your style because of

it, simply stand back and take notice of what you respond to subconsciously. Try going through a stack of magazines and tear out what you are attracted to and group the images in folders labelled 'Bedroom', 'Living Room', 'Kitchen' and so on, to start a visual compilation of what pushes your decorating buttons. You will soon build up an idea of what you're visually responding to so that you can identify your style. You can then begin to personalize the way you live in order to enjoy a down-to-earth honest lifestyle that fits your emotional, physical and spiritual needs.

It's helpful as you examine your clippings to add notes to them identifying exactly what you like about the space. Maybe you only like one thing in the entire image – the chair, or the fireplace mantel and how it is styled. It's important to identify

Sweet and feminine This loose arrangement is the jumping-off point for a guest bedroom doubling as a craft room. Existing furniture will be used and only a new chair will be purchased so the focus is on adding accessories and creating cosy charm. It's all in the details: silk throw cusions, patterned cotton bedding, soft colours and a focus on handmade, tactile finds.

what you like about a magazine tear sheet as this helps you to identify themes in your thinking. Anyone can tap into their inner decorator and make their home a confident reflection of self, whether it is a rental or a sprawling home by the sea, simply through knowing what they like and why and how they respond to these personal favourites.

Stay on the look-out for that 'ah-ha' moment when you walk into a space and instantly feel connected – whether energized or calmed. It could be a home but not always, as inspiring interiors are all around you, from stores to hotel lobbies, cafés to museums. Think about your favourite movies and why you loved the look and feel of them. Record these findings as you go – you will begin to recognize definite patterns in your thinking that will lead you to setting your true decorating style.

'Research is essential in creating a space that reflects your essence. Buy or borrow magazines and tear out what speaks to you; don't think, just feel. Store in your Style File.'

Carrie McCarthy, author

'It's easier than ever to find inspiration because it's so abundant on design blogs. If you can find a blogger whose taste is similar to your own, they'll do the hard work of sourcing things and finding new ideas for you!' *Nicole Balch., blogger*

Danish romantic Let your travels inspire you. This compilation of elements will ultimately result in a living room scheme based on a weekend spent in Copenhagen. Soft linen pillows with a metallic sheen, vintage family photos, tactile throw rugs and storage baskets along with a slip-covered sofa in white and a floor plan will help create a cosy Danish-inspired retreat.

How Mood Boards Work

Many designers turn to mood boards (also referred to as inspiration or concept boards) to convey the overall feel of a project, a visual representation of how they've interpreted their client's requests. By carefully gathering elements in one place, they are able to communicate their concepts more specifically, receive targeted feedback as they progress and deliver focused results. Mood boards can aid not only professional designers but also those who want to tap into their personal style and embark on a decorating project on their own. They expedite the decision-making process and prevent shopping without purpose, which can derail a project and impact negatively on the budget. A mood board can spark creativity, stimulate the imagination, organize ideas and define a palette.

'Pay attention to movies: *Out of Africa* and *Marie Antoinette* have both been a source of great inspiration for me.'

Rachel Ashwell, designer

Use pages from magazines, textile samples, paint swatches, postcards, holiday souvenirs or anything else that speaks to you. Try not to pull from a single catalogue or magazine; you want to create your own vision. A mood board often works best on the wall because it not only serves as a frame of reference but also allows spontaneous editing as your project evolves (if you do not have wall space you can also use a large journal). Pull from your files and pin up elements that speak to you. Pair the overall decorating style that you will use – cottage, eclectic, mid-century, contemporary, bohemian – with the feeling you would like to convey. Place notes on your board that will inspire the design, such as 'restful', 'welcoming', 'natural'. Sketch a floor plan and show some of your favourite furniture and accessories, flooring or wallpaper. You can even pin up found objects, such as a leaf, a tassel from a trip to Marrakech or cherished vintage family photos. Anything goes!

Your ideas can be translated in two ways: inspirational and literal. Purchasing the exact duvet you found in a bedding catalogue is literal. Translating a tiered skirt from a fashion magazine into a ruffled duvet is inspirational.

It can be quite a process to build and edit a mood board, so be patient and give yourself time. On the other hand, it's important to set a deadline to avoid lingering as well as over-editing so that you do not lose your original vision. Often your initial instincts and feelings best define the direction of the space. Remember, designing a mood board and translating it into a finished room scheme are two very different things. To see how your ideas will work in the space, take some elements from the board into the room. For example, drape pieces of fabric on furniture, pin up wallpaper samples, paint a few poster boards and affix them to the wall to see how they look. Leave them in the room for a few days to see how the colours and textures change throughout the day depending on the light. This exercise will provide you with valuable insight so that you can either move forward or rethink your ideas.

BE YOUR OWN CLIENT

When a designer initially consults with a client several questions are asked before a project can begin. After considering these, you can begin to build your mood board.

What is my budget? Do I need to hire help? What is my deadline? Who else should be involved in the decision-making process?

How will I use the space? Will it be for eating, sleeping, working? Will children or pets regularly use the room?

How do I want it to feel? What story would I like to tell? What decorating style best fits my vision?

Will I change the wall colour or flooring? What colours speak to me? Have I checked my colour palette first in natural light?

What architectural considerations should I keep in mind? Do I need to conceal a bad window view? What needs to be changed before I can get started? What do I want to highlight that is currently in the room? What will be the focal point?

What items would I like to have on display and how? Do I need storage? For what? Do I have things in other rooms or in storage that I can incorporate?

What do I need to purchase right away? What can I purchase later, depending on my budget? What can I keep in the room? What can I transform and use in a new way?

Remember . . . Be honest, build your mood board over time, set a deadline and put your plans into action!

COLLECTING YOUR THOUGHTS As you build your palette, lay out your inspirations from paint swatches to fabrics and little details that speak to you and tell a personal story.

PULLING IT ALL TOGETHER
After laying out your inspirations, pin the different elements to your mood board to see how they interact.

Violet Blue

Violet

Violet

Lilac

coBalt
Violet

Turkian Purple

Magenta

TRY OUT IN SITU Next, put your ideas into action. This mood board is for a home office that happens to be in a pool house in the backyard. Still in the beginning stages, the board was brought into the room to see how the colours and textures worked in the space.

'When you create a collage you literally become the designer of your life. You can be selective, creative and intentional in creating your imaginary space. These visuals reflect your essence – look for common threads among the things you love. This will help you translate your taste into wise and beautiful decorating choices.'

Carrie McCarthy, author

SIMPLE STYLE

Simple Style embraces restraint rather than eccentricity, calm rather than clutter and plain tones rather than lots of strong colour. A simply styled room will often include white space furnished with wood and soft neutrals, with the visual interest supplied by a few key pieces of furniture. Layering different textures and combining a number of different materials, such as metal, wood and linen for instance, also brings life to a neutral space. Display and a few dashes of greenery in the form of small house plants make good finishing touches.

On Fyn island near Odense Tine Kjeldsen, owner and designer of homewares brand Tine K Home, has created a smart yet relaxed family home based purely around subtle shades of white mixed with textured woods on furniture and accessories. The neutral palette is extended with shades of grey on picture frames and layers of white and dusky grey on the sofa, chair and cushions.

All of the woodwork is white, including the white-rimmed wall prints and the standard lamp, but it wasn't always so. When renovations started, Tine had new pine floors laid throughout the house. At first they were painted a dark chocolate brown. 'Although they looked very smart, we quickly realized that they just soaked up too much of our northern light and were also difficult to keep in pristine condition. Next, I decided to paint them a pale watery grey colour, in keeping with the nature outside the back door, so we painted them over in white first, which reminded us of the floors in our summerhouse. We liked them so much that we still have them, 18 months on. They wear surprisingly well but we encourage people to walk around in the house without shoes, so that helps reduce scratch marks and general wear and tear.'

'My design ethos is one of mixing different styles and eras, but it has to be done gently, so as not to jar. I love a mix of Far Eastern styles with Scandinavian materials, colour and shapes.'

Tine Kjeldsen

WHITE SYMPHONY An overall white scheme increases the sense of space in this narrow living room, where the natural light bounces off the glossy floor and pale surfaces. Comfort comes in textured fabrics and plenty of lanterns and candlelight.

'The furniture has evolved over time,' says Tine. 'I like to combine elements of my own Tine K Home collection with one-off pieces sourced from antique shops and junk stores in nearby Odense and elsewhere.' In the living room the coffee table was bought in Vietnam, while in the dining room the Chinese cupboard came from the Danish boutique Suzanne Varming.

Layering whites on walls, floors and woodwork, then combining them with Tine's favourite soft neutral colours creates an atmosphere of harmony and laid-back chic. The slightly battered wooden tables tie the scheme together and lend warmth and patina to the clean whites elsewhere in the space.

NEUTRAL COLLECTION *Left* A display cabinet from Vietnam is the perfect showcase for a collection of vintage books and basketware, while the glossy white wooden floor is a sophisticated anchor for pure white walls and a small evergreen tree.

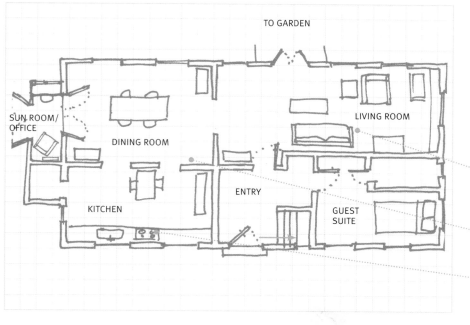

TO GARDEN

SUN ROOM/ OFFICE

DINING ROOM

LIVING ROOM

KITCHEN

ENTRY

GUEST SUITE

Mixed and matched Far Eastern furniture placed against white and pale upholstery gives a clean-lined simplicity.

White floors throughout enhances the sense of space.

A simple kitchen layout means the rest of the room is given over to display and a small work table.

'The colours I love to work with are pale grey, blue and lots of white, in many different shades.'

Tine Kjeldsen

NATURAL DINING East meets West in the dining room, where Tine had her large wooden dining table custom made so as to contrast with the Vietnamese plain wood tables elsewhere in the house. One of the chairs is painted grey for an unexpected touch.

'To be able to open the terrace doors every day during the spring and summer is fantastic. With three children who love nature, the huge garden is a gift.'

Tine Kjeldsen

'I have collected cabinets and small tables over a period of time. Many of them come from a small antique shop in Odense that I'm always taking a trip to.'

Tine Kjeldsen

CREATIVE NOOK *This page*
A makeshift trestle table fits snugly Into a small sunroom to create a delightful place for painting, working or simply enjoying the view.

QUIET CORNER *Opposite*
In the same area a quiet corner is devoted to a cosy chair and a chance for relaxation with a view.

Simple Style Guidelines *Pare down and beautify*

'Keep it simple – in smaller spaces, you should have a unifying colour scheme, and not too much pattern, otherwise it will make you crazy.' *Tom Delavan, designer*

1 SIMPLICITY RULES
Keeping it simple is one way to maximize a sense of space in a small home. Cutting down on accessories, wall adornment and busy colour or pattern will clear not only the clutter but also the senses.

2 SIMPLE COLOURS
Start off by working with a colour palette that includes only two or three core colours and mix and match these across walls, floors, furniture and furnishings.

3 NATURAL NEUTRALS
Natural materials often fit well in a simple space. Bamboo, wood, leather, cotton and linen all look at home in spaces that take white and off-white as their colour cue.

4 VISUAL INTEREST
Use materials, textures and details to provide a shot of colour here or layers of texture there to build up a look of only a few elements but a lot of visual interest.

5 SEEK INSPIRATION
Find great simple ideas by looking at seaside homes in the Hamptons or lakeside cabins in Scandinavia. Paint wood on walls and floors, or seek out furniture in simple shapes or interesting materials.

MATERIAL EFFECTS Use lampshades to complement materials elsewhere in the room. Here ruched silk lampshades echo perfectly the broken lines of bamboo dining chairs in Tine Kjeldsen's Danish home.

WHITE CHINA White-on-white displays never fail to delight the senses and lend a sense of calm to a space. Choose china, paper-covered books, framed photographs or flowers for creating a display.

'Beautiful materials used simply are luxurious – cotton and linen for crisp coolness, wool for sustainable warmth and comfort. For furniture and furnishings, used in a pared down way stripes can be either contemporary or classic.' *Roger Oates, designer*

6 DETAILING Use details to echo colours or objects elsewhere in a room. A simple striped cushion may have a couple of large dark wooden buttons as detailing that echo a dark wooden floor or table elsewhere in the room.

7 FUNCTION AND STYLE Keep an emphasis on function in simple spaces. You won't need overly complicated window treatments or sofas with curlicued legs. Similarly avoid busy patterned wallpaper or textiles.

8 LIGHTING Simple lighting can work wonders in keeping a space warm but appealing. Include floor-standing lamps next to a sofa, or adjustable ceiling overhead glass pendants above a dining table.

9 FURNITURE Create a mix of clean-lined pieces in smart but simple fabrics – cool linens, textured plains or subtle stripes all work in simple settings. You can always jazz up the seating with interesting cushions.

10 SIMPLE STORAGE Having enough storage is important in simple style. Don't put too much on display and make sure that clutter lives behind closed doors, in the form of discreet built-in solutions.

CHIC BATHROOM White units and dark brown detailing work well against walls that are painted palest grey and a pale stone floor. Experiment with pale neutral tester pots to get your optimum shade.

DESIGNER DETAIL We love these simple bespoke leather handles as a way of livening up plain and simple bathroom cupboard doors. You could also choose zinc handles or ceramic knobs instead.

Why White Works

White is the favourite colour of many a professional decorator. It always looks clean, bright, calm and allows you endless opportunities for playing with colour, scale and texture.

1 In this New York loft white walls and floors allow light to flood in. Black woodwork is echoed in the metal plinths of large planters either side of a Perspex chair. Transparent furniture works well in white spaces and enhances the light that dances in.

'After experimenting with many colours of paint I always come back to white walls because I like how art looks on a brighter white wall.'

*Leslie Shewring,
photographer/stylist*

2 In kitchens and bathrooms, white tiles are always a good choice. Glossy surfaces help reflect light in darker spaces and always look smart and inviting, particularly against steel fixtures and fittings.

4 The classic monochrome colour scheme is always pleasing and never dull. Crisp dark lines of picture frames against white walls with dark furniture is an easy look to achieve and comfortable to live with.

3 Taking an all-white approach to bedrooms allows you to clear your head, both visually and mentally after a busy day, allowing you to focus on simple pleasures and rest.

5 Strip down reclaimed cupboards and paint them white inside and out to create a beautiful display case. Add shelf detailing or wallpaper panels at the back if you want decorative touches.

2

3

4

5

NATURAL STYLE

Natural may imply neutral but it certainly doesn't mean bland. This mix of modern and classical design takes its cue from natural, reclaimed and salvaged materials and a fondness for white.

In their Brooklyn brownstone, metalsmith and designer Lyndsay Caleo and sculptor and designer Fitzhugh Karol say 'There is a story behind everything that we have in our house. When we moved in we had no furniture other than a wood bookshelf that Lyndsay had built a few years before. We had access to many large logs though. There was an ice storm one winter and a landscaper we knew had more logs than he knew what to do with. We spent the summer after graduating designing and building our furniture and looking on internet auction sites for everything else . . . like our kitchen sink,' explains Fitzhugh.

'Our palette is primarily white as there is nothing more beautiful or invigorating. It's like waking up every day to a clean slate,' says Lyndsay. The couple first saw the home, built in the late 1800s, when it had rotten floors, fire damage and the horrendous remnants of a late 1970s renovation. Despite this, the house felt just right to them and they set about restoring rooms.

'I would definitely recommend painting floors white, but only if you can relax and appreciate a little wear and tear,' advises Lyndsay. 'The light you get is amazing. We recommend using a hard-wearing non-oil-based deck-floor paint from a marine supply store.'

SALVAGED SHELVES Storm-damaged timber was used to form rough and ready shelves, with metal brackets designed by Lyndsay. Plenty of texture is important in natural decorating.

ECO ETHOS For a great natural look mix high with low, new modern with handmade and hunt around for great objects and fixtures.

'Our home is a living sketchbook, full of our design experiments and ideas, and holds our ever-changing displays of books, artwork, furniture and objects that inspire and motivate us.' *Lyndsay Caleo and Fitzhugh Karol*

WOOD AND WHITE The ceiling beams were covered up for a hundred years. Now they give the room great texture to counterpoint the neutral colour scheme.

FOUR POSTER Fitzhugh hand carved wood to form the four-poster in the bedroom.

KITCHEN AREA

LIVING AREA

BATH ROOM

BEDROOM

DINING AREA

SLEEPING AREA ABOVE

ENTRY

The kitchen sink was the starting point for the pair's home and they went on to design and make other elements as the space evolved. The barn door on the bathroom was an early acquisition too. 'Rooms and collections evolve and when they do, they look much more natural,' says Lyndsay. 'We like to make every bit of space useful.'

The salvaged sink was the starting point for the entire decorative scheme.

A table from recycled wood and reclaimed furniture make for a truly sustainable living space.

A hand-carved four poster bed made from reclaimed wood is the key feature in the bedoom.

WARM WOOD
The salvaged barn door that leads to the bathroom reflects the style of the whole house, which has an air of calm but warm simplicity and a close relationship with eco-friendly materials.

'The best rooms in a home are always evolving.
Mix it up and only bring into your home things
that you love.' *Lyndsay Caleo*

Natural Style Guidelines *Reclaim, restore and reconnect*

'Reuse, repair and recycle! Stop throwing things away and get out of the disposable mindset. Take a leaf out of our grandparents' books. Get creative with the abandoned, broken and unloved.' *Atlanta Bartlett, designer*

IT'S GOOD TO GO GREEN Introducing a natural take in your home can range from upcycling furniture to choosing environmentally friendly fixtures and fittings and working with eco fabrics.

WOOD, WOOD, WOOD The cornerstone of natural inspiration, wood works wonders on floors, furniture, one-off pieces such as tree trunk tables or driftwood sculptures. Teamed with white walls or floors, wood warms a room.

INSPIRATION Stools and benches made from complete tree branches and twigs, witty twig stools and chairs plus bamboo dining chairs and bed frames in clean-lined bamboo are all interesting in a cool, natural space.

NATURAL PALETTE From the vivid lichen greens of a forest backdrop to the white and off-white palette of chalky neutrals and the coastal neutrals of blues, greys and bluff white, the natural palette need not be all brown and white.

TEXTURES AND LAYERS Texture is important in a natural palette, whether the rich patina of worn wood or the reassuring warmth of wool and linen, or the scrupulous simplicity of Egyptian cotton, calico or scrim.

RECYCLED SHELVING Reclaimed wood is ideal for small shelving projects, in the kitchen, living room or bedroom. Even better are bespoke metal or wooden brackets to support your display.

GO GREEN Delightful unbleached cotton cushions with greenery motifs in a soft autumn green colour are the perfect idea for a white sofa dressed with a boiled wool throw.

'Natural objects are always very welcome in my home. Some people view some of my finds as trash but for me they are treasures. It's all about changing the lens you use to look at them.' *Fernanda Bourlot, designer*

6 FURNITURE Generous sofas, chunky tree-trunk stools and banquettes and carefully streamlined contemporary pieces made from elegant ash or birch all resonate well in a natural space.

7 REUSE AND RECLAIM Keep an eye out for old wooden fruit crates for storing everything from craft supplies to children's toys, magazines to clothes. Old glass-fronted cupboards are also great for storage and display.

8 KEEPING IT SMART The William Morris ethos of useful and beautiful chimes well with the natural ethos. Mix high design with low handmade items for a pleasing juxtaposition and strong visual interest.

9 FLOORING Keep walls and floors relatively plain and let the textures do the talking. Painted, stained or stripped wooden flooring is the classic natural solution; other choices include seagrass matting and linoleum.

10 LIGHTING The most natural lighting of all is candlelight, so make sure to incorporate some candles, whether large chunky church candles or delicate tea lights placed in metal and glass storm lanterns.

PERSONAL COLLECTION Lyndsay Caleo and Fitzhugh Karol designed and built not only their storage and display system but also their dining table too. Discreet cupboards hide less aesthetic belongings.

NATURAL GLAMOUR A reclaimed door adds instant warmth to the bathroom where smart retro fittings sit on a warming cork floor, which is both eco-friendly, economical and hardwearing.

Sustainable Living

Reclaiming and reusing materials is as much a matter of necessity as it is of eco-aesthetics, since preserving the earth's natural resources is high on people's personal agendas.

1 Fitzhugh Karol used storm-damaged timber to create a bed frame, a lamp base and a tree-trunk table in his TV room. Timber yards are always happy to sell you offcuts of timber if you want to get creative with wood.

2 Baths can be reclaimed and reconditioned so they are fit for purpose. Sometimes the worn, peeling look becomes part of the ethos. In a converted industrial building, traditional elements echo the age of the building.

3 Ingrid Jansen's delightful stools are made from recycled timber and topped with pretty crocheted wool covers for a look that is both pleasingly handcrafted and eco-conscious.

4 In a smart, minimal home, discarded fruit crates are both warming for the space and a fun means of storing craft materials.

5 Vintage and retro storage pieces and furniture always add tons of personality to a space as well as a happy mix of interesting materials.

'I think it's clearly easier than ever before to find eco-friendly furniture and accessories for your home – whether it's bamboo, Forest Stewardship Council approved wood pieces or even just picking up things from a flea market or thrift shop to reuse them.'

Danny Seo, green living expert

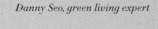

2

3

4

5

'We knocked down
the walls on the
ground floor to
turn three small
rooms into a
huge kitchen and
dining space.'

Virginia Armstrong

MODERN STYLE

Modern style has a lot to do with a clean, uncluttered vibe, a muted sense of colour that is restrained yet sophisticated and fabulous elegant mid-century classic furniture such as Ercol sofas and Danish modern circular dining tables. Mid-century furniture is universally admired and relatively easy to obtain, either in its original form or as reproduction pieces.

Designer Virginia Armstrong runs textile and print company Roddy & Ginger out of her south-east London base, where she has created a beautiful yet functional family home taking mid-century modern style as the starting point for her decorating ideas. 'It's a great family home on five floors and I have the luxury of a basement room that I use as my studio and workshop.'

CLEAN LINES
Mismatched mid-century classic chairs around a Saarinen Tulip table provide stylish seating at the family dining table. Light, space and a functional kitchen all reflect modern style.

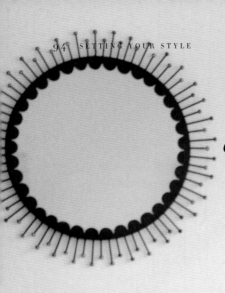

'I love chairs. Some
of my favourite
possessions are my
vintage chairs.
And my Ercol sofa is
special because of its
lovely elegant shape.'

Virginia Armstrong

PURE AND SIMPLE
In a pure white space
Virginia Armstrong has
created visual interest and
harmony by mixing woods
with a soft colour palette of
turquoise blues and fern.

ON THE SIDE Several Danish furniture companies, such as France & Son and Vinde Møbelfabrik, produced sideboards such as this in the 1950s and 60s. Sturdily made from teak or rosewood, they are both practical and beautiful.

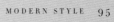

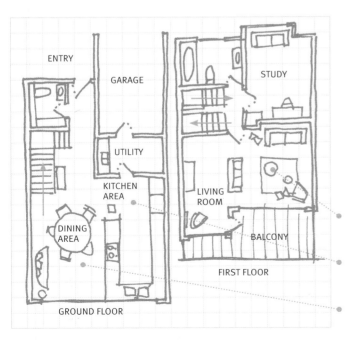

ENTRY

GARAGE

STUDY

UTILITY

KITCHEN AREA

LIVING ROOM

DINING AREA

BALCONY

FIRST FLOOR

GROUND FLOOR

'We chose the house because it was large and light, with huge windows and was a very good price,' says Virginia. 'Slowly people have come to realize the amazing potential of 1960s suburban homes and their suitability to mid-century modern style. We have set about transforming the house into a modern space using key pieces of mid-century furniture collected over the years. The great thing about this classic furniture is its durability and practicality so for once it is quite easy to assimilate collectable designer furniture into a family home.'

Mid-century furniture needs space around it so the clean-lined aesthetic can be viewed from all angles.

The kitchen is very simply styled and incorporates a room divider/ worktop area so as not to detract from the dining area.

The dining space, with its Eero Saarinen Tulip table and Ercol sofa demands the main visual attention on the ground floor.

Modern Style Guidelines *All that's hip and happening*

'I love modern classic design, its beauty and charisma, which doesn't go out of date. High-quality manufacturing guarantees a long life expectancy too.' *Claudia Nowotny, store owner*

CHAIRS Some of the classics are now very pricey but get the look by buying some reproduction pieces if necessary. Look out for the key Scandinavian designers and their signature pieces.

FURNITURE Sturdy sideboards, kidney-shaped occasional tables, single and in nests, and clean-lined rosewood and teak Danish coffee tables are all key elements in any modern style interior.

CERAMICS Make an instant statement by displaying a small tea service or some storage jars from the 1950s–1970s. These can still be found at retro junk stalls and charity or thrift stores.

GRAPHIC PATTERNS On textiles used for curtain fabrics or upholstery, graphic shapes and motifs in colours such as brown, dusky orange and forest green are all recognizably modern style.

SCANDINAVIAN INFLUENCE Danish Modern style provided the life force for stylized wood-framed furniture and lighting, and wood was a key material even for smaller items, such as bowls and candle holders.

COOL MIDWINTER Group together a collection of white ceramics from a particular era in the middle part of the last century and enjoy their different shapes, styles and forms.

KEEP IT CLEAN In a modern space, allow materials to do the talking. Simple wooden furniture and a stripped floor and staircase provide a neutral space in which jolts of colour provide the visual interest.

'Mid-century furniture feels fresh and optimistic. It comes from a period of time when designers were thinking to the future, not the past, and saying how can we do things differently?' *Amy Butler, designer*

6 LIGHTING There are so many key designs and so many contemporary reproductions to choose from that you can easily lift the look and translate it to any room in the house.

7 FLOORING AND RUGS Plain wooden floorboards are de rigeur for modern style. Dress the space with bold and colourful graphic rugs to add some warmth and comfort in rooms that are often wood and white in style.

8 GLASS Bold, colourful glass in smoky browns, blues, purples and turquoise are unmistakably modern; from apothecary-style glass vials to 1960s flat glass ashtrays and bulbous vases, build up a display.

9 STUDYING THE STYLE Visit 20th-century design museums for inspiration and to view work of the key designers. From Amsterdam and London to Florida and Copenhagen, the ideas will soon flow.

10 CHROME AND STEEL Tubular steel is often used on furniture legs and on lights. The classic Arco lamp is made from stainless steel and shiny steel vases will tie in to a wood and chrome scheme.

TIME FOR TEA Mass-produced 1960s china, with its graphic patterns and simple shapes, is enjoying a revival amid the vintage and retro movement of preserving rather than consuming.

RETRO READS Vintage books with distinctive dust jackets are delightful objects in their own right, whether used for reading, displaying or as sources of inspiration for decorating.

Mid-Century Classic Furniture

The shapes and forms of mid-century furniture are not only collectors' items and the antiques of the future, but have also inspired new interpretations of classic designs and reissues of the work of several master designers.

I Amy Butler's cool dining space includes a round table that is reminiscent of Eero Saarinen's classic Tulip table, while a sideboard is home to a collection of vintage glassware.

2 Wirework chairs such as this 1960s classic still look completely contemporary, wherever you choose to put them – kitchen, living room or dining space.

3 The classic Ercol wooden-framed sofa has never gone out of fashion, seldom wears out and is currently being reissued as a design classic.

4 A Saarinen Tulip table original, complete with reupholstered chairs, proves that modern design and a traditional room can live happily together.

5 Poul Kjaerholm's classic Scandinavian modern dining chairs retain their elegance and simplicity at a modern zinc table.

I

2

3

4

5

'A home takes time to grow and become personal. I think this can only be done over years, collecting interesting bits and bobs from holidays, car boot sales and junk shops. Then your character starts to shine through and the house begins to reflect your personality.'

Sania Pell

JUNK MAGIC Old haberdasher's storage drawers and a reupholstered sofa are set off well with a still-life display of ceramic vases and a vintage industrial clock.

ATTIC CONVERSION A comfortable armchair has been re-covered with linen and embellished with handcut floral fabric motifs and velvet offcuts.

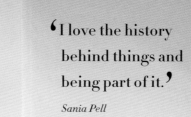

'I love the history behind things and being part of it.'

Sania Pell

FLEA MARKET STYLE

Whether you call it junk, garage sale style or simply 'old stuff', there's no doubt that flea market chic's time is now. While the world has realized that recycling and reusing is not only a virtue but also a necessity for the sake of the planet, the idea of living with second-hand furniture and objects is as fashionable as the latest Paris catwalk show.

Those in the know can be found in thrift stores and flea markets rather than high-end furniture showrooms, seeking out a 1930s clock or a 1970s tea service, a 1960s wood-framed sofa or a much loved but slightly battered painting to add character and personality to their home.

Sania Pell, stylist and writer, specializes in the handmade object and has spent a long time collecting and displaying interesting utility items in her London home. 'I love anything that is handmade, eclectic, graphic or quirky,' she

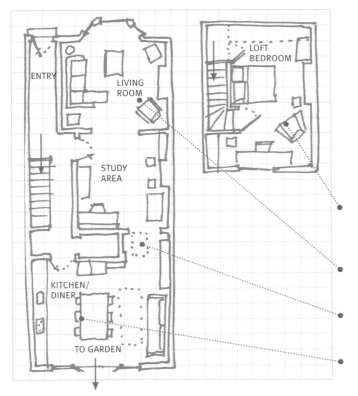

says. 'When we bought our 100-year-old home it had been unloved so it was up to us to realize its potential and to inject some soul into it. We like to update and transform furniture that has been given to us, or to revamp older pieces in a new way. The 1930s chair in the living room was given to my husband's grandmother as a wedding present. When she gave it to us it was covered with purple nylon – very 1970s retro. We re-covered it in a grey bouclé and it was instantly transformed into something different and special.'

There are many pieces of furniture, objects and artworks, but it is all family-proof. Nothing is too precious that it requires the children to be especially careful.

Every inch of the house is used; there is no sacred space saved for special occasions only.

The living room is devoted to displays of flea market finds that have a common colour theme with the rest of the room: tan, black or white.

Extending into a side alley and putting in a wall of glass doors doubles the size of the kitchen.

STILL LIFE Favourite utility objects arranged as a still life lend character and vitality to a home.

'Some of my favourite possessions are objects made or drawn by other people, especially my 6-year-old son. Others are finds from art degree shows or craft fairs.'

Sania Pell

A HANDMADE HOME Surrounding yourself with handmade items collected over time is a great way of bringing the past up to date.

06

'We like collecting old utility items and displaying them, like the antique rulers and surveying staffs, for example, and old cricket scoreboard numbers and signs.' *Sania Pell*

Flea Market Style Guidelines *Furnish with found objects*

'I always carry a kind of mental list in my head of things I am looking for as I often find something beautiful when I least expect it.' *Atlanta Bartlett, designer*

1 DISPLAY Flea market finds always look good on display. Highlight them by placing objects on a plain white windowsill or bookcase or meld them into a piece of junk furniture such as pigeon-hole shelving or utility shop fittings.

2 QUIRKY STORAGE Find common but discarded objects such as fruit crates and use them for storage, or convert wooden pallets into coffee tables by adding castors underneath.

3 COLLECTIONS Spending happy times in flea markets and junk shops often leads to building a collection of items you may never have encountered before. Celebrate the beauty of old fruit box labels or enamel kitchenalia.

4 UPCYCLING Take a piece of retro furniture and either paint or decorate it to make it unique. Change the handles, add tassels instead of draw pulls, resurface a table with mirror or marble or re-upholster a sofa with jute or retro fabric.

5 TALKING-POINT PIECES Seek out interesting one-off pieces to add drama to your space. It could be a wirework dressmaker's dummy, a freestanding ceramic animal, a discarded store display item or a garden sculpture.

DESIGNER KEYS Use smaller flea market finds to embellish existing items such as a lampshade. Here vintage keys are ranged around a plain lampshade to give a quirky edging.

BE A CURATOR Arrange your flea market discoveries in a considered way and have fun with placing furniture and lights close to art on the walls to create the look.

'I start at the back of a flea market and work my way forward. I like to think everyone else is still browsing the front rows and if I start backwards I might score a great treasure no one has seen yet.' *Victoria Smith, blogger*

6 LIGHTING You will find examples of great chandeliers, floor and table lamps from the 1930s onwards with which to furnish your space. If you only choose one light make it a chandelier, either frilly or functional.

7 PICTURES Arranging a display of framed pictures throws up an infinite number of possibilities for personalizing your space. Paint the frames one colour and fill them with faded landscapes or stylized flower paintings.

8 SOURCING Say the words flea market and instantly the Sunday morning markets of Paris spring to mind. The fact is there are now flea markets everywhere. Take time to visit a few and you will quickly establish a network of favourites.

9 MIXING AND MATCHING The great mantra of mixing old and new to create something personal is particularly pertinent to flea market style. Revel in mixing up the eras and playing with colours and materials.

10 USING INSTINCT If your eye fixes on a battered cabinet across a crowded junk shop floor then you'll find it hard to go home without it. Trust your instinct and buy only items that you are really attracted to from the start.

JEWELLERY STORE A pair of discarded jewellery store display hands make a great feature on a chunky shelf, especially when put to their original purpose as jewellery stands.

CUSTOMIZED DISPLAY Shop-bought storage cubes have been decorated with flea market stickers and graphics and a noticeboard created to match for a workstation. Economic but stylish.

Flea Market Finds

Decorating with flea market finds often means finding a single item that sparks your imagination in different directions. It may be fabric, furniture, mirrors or even vintage clothing that set you off.

I In Emily Chalmers' industrial loft, the mid-century furniture and vintage textiles combine to create a welcoming, quirky space.

2 Retro mirrors in a tiny kitchen create a vintage feel that is smart rather than strictly nostalgic.

3 Gather together a collection of vases and vessels from the same decorative period but in different colours for a bright display. Fill them with twigs and dried flowers in winter and vivid flowers in summer.

4 A metal shelving unit is filled with functional but decorative items to make a great wall display. Oriental food packets, brightly coloured condiment bottles and tableware all bring colour.

5 Enamel advertising signs bring an instant sense of flea market style to a space. Search out ones that complement other furniture finds you have in the room.

2

3

4

5

CASE STUDY

COLOURFUL STYLE

Decorating with colour is one of the most personal styles of decorating you can undertake. One person's favourite vivid turquoise or sugar plum pink can be another's idea of excess in the taste department, while a pale neutral palette beloved of many professional decorators may seem like a bland compromise to those who love bolds and brights. The important thing is to take a good look around you, in magazines, at homes you love and while out shopping, to get an idea of what colours you are instantly attracted to.

Colour means everything to Alayne Patrick, owner of the fashion and home interiors store, Layla, in Brooklyn. She describes her Brooklyn home as small but efficient, but with the unusual and enviable bonus of an outdoor space, where she has created a bright, cheerful seating area that brings a touch of Asian influence to the city.

'Don't be afraid of colour and mix prints up to create impact.' *Alayne Patrick*

ASIAN COOL Vibrant fuchsia fabrics on cushions and rugs provide a sharp contrast to rich verdant greens and sunny yellows elsewhere in this colourful living room.

GLOBAL CHIC A vintage iron bedstead is decorated with Asian embroidered and hand-blocked cushions and pillows and other ethnic fabrics, while the art on the walls is whimsical and feminine.

'I am inspired by anything Asian, Indian and colourful that is handmade and good quality, whether it's old or new,' says Alayne, who has managed to inject strong flourishes of colour into her home by the clever use of textiles. 'My sofa was the first piece of furniture I bought when I came to live in New York. I found it in a vintage furniture store and it's been completely refurbished since. Some furniture I have had custom-made to fit the apartment because of its limited dimensions.

'In the bedroom I used thick black tape on the walls as a border to define the sleep space. This is something I've seen a lot in India, where of course it is usually handpainted, but I've always wanted to use this device in my own home.' It provides graphic definition in the white space, rather like a dado rail would.

'I would love to have a bigger, separate bedroom but the space constraints at least make me tidy. However, I dream of more closets, especially a walk-in one to store my clothing, fabrics and linens.'

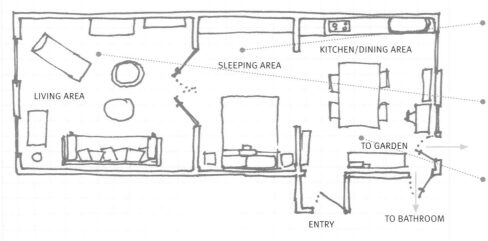

LIVING AREA

SLEEPING AREA

KITCHEN/DINING AREA

TO GARDEN

ENTRY

TO BATHROOM

- The entire space is only 46m² (495ft²) and consists of three connecting square rooms – a kitchen, bedroom/bathroom and a living room.

- Mix up colours and patterns but keep furniture to the minimum.

- Comfortable seating in every room, including the outdoor space, creates a cosy vibe.

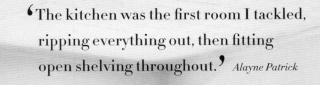

'The kitchen was the first room I tackled, ripping everything out, then fitting open shelving throughout.' *Alayne Patrick*

COLOURFUL DINING
Ethnic fabrics are used to brighten up the neat kitchen/diner and instil colour into the neutral space.

'Among my favourite possessions are my embroidered dowry pillows from the Swat region of Pakistan.' *Alayne Patrick*

BESPOKE DAY BED It's a good idea to consider having pieces of furniture custom-made when space is tight.

OUTDOOR LIVING The outdoor space is as big again as the apartment, so throw rugs layered on the concrete surface warm up the area, making it an inviting extension of the apartment.

'It was the garden and the kitchen that first attracted me to this place. I've made the garden into an outdoor room so that the living space can spill outside when the weather is good.' *Alayne Patrick*

Colourful Style Guidelines *Embolden your home*

'Bold, blingy and fabulous: nothing changes the personality of a space like colour. It seduces, thrills and surprises and adds high voltage energy to any room. Overdose on it I say!' *Abigail Ahern, designer*

CHOOSING A PALETTE Work with colours you love and you will always be pleased with the end result. Don't be afraid to experiment too, though. Look at colour combinations you respond to.

BLANKET COVERAGE You may want to drench a room in a particular shade to create drama and impact. From sugar plum pink to electric blue, rooms that shout colour can be fun to create.

COLOURFUL WALLS Painting a single wall is a good way to go if you want to try out a new colour to see whether you can live with it. A wall painted up to dado height in a vivid colour with white above it is a way to live with some colour.

ALL IN THE DETAIL Introducing colour via details that can switch around is both versatile and creative. Look at what you have and how you mix and match items to create a colour story.

LIGHTING Use either lampshades or colourful light bulbs in wall uplighters to inject colour into your surroundings at night. Coloured glass chandeliers will also throw off different tones and textures of light.

DELICATE CHINA Ceramics decorated with motifs of burnt orange, faded yellow and soft pinks and plums echo colours used elsewhere in Alayne Patrick's textile-inspired Brooklyn home.

PATTERN AND TEXTURE Layering cushions and textiles on beds and sofas is a great way to decorate a space, especially if walls and floors are plain. Mix textured fabrics with florals and embroidered surfaces.

'I have always had a fascination with colour. I truly love all colours. For me, it is more about the intensity of a colour, rather than the hue itself. A monochromatic room can evoke harmony while a room full of brilliant hues can be energizing.' *Kelly Wearstler, designer*

FLOORS Painted floors can be just as dramatic as painted walls. Colourful tones can be enhanced and emboldened by the addition of crisp, bright rugs or even painted stripes.

TEXTILES The perfect way to both soften and decorate a room is by using textiles on upholstery, at the windows or as tablecloths. Layer patterns, textures and colours to create a huge range of styles.

FLOWERS Use flowers to either create colour, complement an existing scheme or start a bold colour clash in a room. Use a variety of vases in differing heights and styles in which to introduce the colour.

FURNITURE Treat your furniture to a colour makeover, whether by changing the upholstery or painting it to blend in with your scheme. It can be the central colour focus of the room or else a backdrop to colourful walls and floors.

SPLASHES OF COLOUR Add a dash of colour by using a bright shade on a tablelamp, painting behind dresser shelves or painting the panels of a door. Tableware is capable of shifting the colour balance, as are bold artworks.

FLOWER MAGIC Combine complementary colours such as green and red to create a lively palette that is bright and welcoming. These fuchsia pink and emerald green cushions make a bold statement.

EVERYDAY TEXTILES Bring colour to your everyday chores by using tea cloths and towels that are brimming with vibrant tones. They will make you smile and add welcome colour to a kitchen or dining area.

Introducing Colour *Brightening your home*

Floors anchor a space so think about whether you want them to recede or intervene in a room by painting them white, keeping them dark or carpeting them in a rich colour.

Create a feature in a white space by painting a wall in a bold colour such as red, blue or orange.

Choose colours that suit your space. White will always enlarge a space. Red is an advancing colour, so will make a small room feel cosy and disguise its size.

Collections of similar-coloured objects will provide visual punctuation in a space. Consider artworks, textiles, ceramics, glass, vases, sculptures, vintage hats, books and suitcases.

Introduce seasonal colour by having a spare set of loose covers for your sofas and chairs. Try white or neutral for summer, and rich reds or browns for winter perhaps.

Wallpaper is a great way of providing colour in a room, either on one feature wall or throughout the room.

Look at accent colours – introduce them incidentally on flowers, lampshades, rugs or soft furnishings.

FLORAL FANCY *Left* In a Belgian living space one wall is given over to a spriggy floral wallpaper to create a feature wall, further accented by cushions on an all-white sofa.

BRIGHT ACCENTS *Opposite* Charlotte Hedeman Gueniau's Danish home has plenty of colour that is provided on movable objects – lampshades, tableware and cushions – so changes can be introduced daily if the mood takes her.

'The more I decorate the more I learn about introducing a complementary colour somewhere, such as throwing a turquoise pillow in an orange room. Always test many colours in every single part of the room.' *Ruthie Sommers, designer*

I

Colourful Furniture

Painted furniture will enliven your room and decorate your space with a minimum of disruption or expense.

'At home I have painted some old vintage wooden dining chairs with neon pink paint. The colour actually makes me feel happy!' *Selina Lake, stylist*

1 Painting an old cabinet in a vivid colour makes for an uplifting colour statement. Bright paint will also disguise any imperfections on furniture that has seen smarter days.

2 In kitchens, consider using colourful appliances in your scheme. A summery pink and blue scheme is achieved here by the use of only two items.

3 Make a big colour statement by using strong colour on both walls and furniture. Here a shocking pink cupboard is a cheerful complement to a bright turquoise blue wall.

4 On the subtle end of the spectrum, duck-egg blue and other neutral-based colours work well on furniture in a traditional setting, creating a quiet and sophisticated palette.

5 Apple green is a joyful colour that works well in white and off-white spaces. Combine it with red curtains for a warming scheme.

2

3

4

5

Colourful Textiles

Dotting colourful textiles throughout a home is a delightful way of injecting life, decoration and a little joyfulness into a space, with florals, stripes, checks or knitted or embroidered pieces.

I This bedroom mixes complementary blue and orange in a variety of patterns and textures to create impact. An orange mohair throw is the icing on the cake.

2 In a tribute to ethnic eco, a variety of colourful handmade textiles on pegs provide a colourful, globetrotting tableau.

3 Mix and match colours in a similar spectrum for a cohesive effect. Here fuchsia, purple and deepest navy work well with cool greys and whites elsewhere in the bedroom.

4 Patchwork on curtains or upholstery is always pleasing on the eye. Theme the patches by subject, such as florals, stripes or geometrics or by fabrics, such as cotton ticking or linens.

5 Stripes and florals often work well together, especially when some colours are repeated from one to the other.

6 Place embroidered fabrics on top of bold colours so that each of the elements make a crisp visual statement, making sure that the embroidery includes some of the bold colours.

'Textiles are the quickest and easiest way to bring style, colour, pattern and texture into a room. Whatever your taste, snuggly throws, cheerful crochet, fabulous fabrics, cosy quilts and squishy cushions are all a gift to the home decorator.' *Jane Brocket, author*

I

4

2

3

5

6

Wallpaper

Using wallpaper to decorate a space has never been more fun to do because there are so many designs and styles to choose from.

1 Make a feminine statement in the bedroom by using delicate floral wallpaper that is as subtle as it is pretty. The wallpaper makes the space but the bed dressing is in keeping with it.

2 This iconic Cole & Son treescape design shows how wallpaper can become the defining feature of a room. It is both decoration and statement rolled into one.

3 Floral papers are enjoying a timely revival and always add warmth and comfort, even if only used on a single wall. This pattern was originally designed by Josef Frank in the 1940s.

4 In a small room, disguise the limited space by applying two different wallpapers to adjacent walls. These Liberty prints are both pretty and stylish.

5 Let the wallpaper do the talking and range it over walls and ceilings to give the impression of a tented space; the effect is bold but beautiful.

6 Classic toile de Jouy designs are always appealing on bedroom walls, giving off a rural vibe, whatever the location of the space.

'Great wallpaper prints give personality in much the same way great paint colours do. It's fashion really. Sometimes you want a solid-coloured skirt, sometimes you go for the beautiful print.' *Amy Butler, designer*

1

4

2

3

5

6

FLORAL STYLE

Decorating using floral motifs isn't always about colour but it can be a great excuse to go bold. Whether it's walls, textiles or ceramics, there are endless variations on the floral theme, from breezy blooms on wallpaper and fabrics to stylized Japanese-inspired blossoms on delicate porcelain china and furniture. Two-tone flowers make quite a subtle statement, while one corner of a room decorated with a floral decal or handpainted with small flowers is a quieter way of going floral.

Charlotte Hedeman Gueniau runs the innovative home furnishings campany, Rice, in Odense, Denmark. When not busy launching new collections or travelling the world gathering inspiration, she likes to spend time with her family in their 19th-century house in Kerteminde, on the island of Fyn, in Denmark.

'It's a great place for indulging my love of bold, zingy colours and florals. I am always at one with the happy colours of pink, green, petrol and yellow. For me grey, beige and black are not even considered a colour. I often let my paintings inspire the colour scheme for a room. In the Fyn house we were attracted by the big space, the good natural light and the generously proportioned rooms. There's also a great view and we're surrounded by beautiful landscape,' explains Charlotte.

'Sometimes colour accidents happen. We had a happy misunderstanding in the TV room. Our painter had applied a bright coral colour on one wall but I meant for him to paint over a petrol-coloured wall elsewhere in the room. In fact, when

FLOWER POWER *Opposite* Raspberry pink gloss units look almost understated against a wall of glorious blousy pink rose wallpaper that brings instant cheer to the kitchen.

'My space is all about fun, function and colours.' *Charlotte Hedeman Gueniau*

COLOURFUL CHINA *This page* Open shelves display a vibrant mix of floral cups and saucers, a vintage tea set and acid bright melamine cups.

I saw the two colours together they really worked. I couldn't stop laughing, but it actually looked great, so we kept it.'

Floral motifs occur throughout several rooms in the house. In the hallway a bright folk-art style motif is used on the wallpaper, while the kitchen is resplendent in bouffant pink roses against a dark background. Rugs and runners all repeat the pink-on-pink floral theme in the kitchen and family room.

In the dining room flowers are present on different floral vases and containers, while real flowers have a permanent place at the table. Flowers also adorn lampshades, crocheted pan holders, tinware and display ceramics in the kitchen, and the guest room has subtle floral wallpaper and cushions in more muted colours. 'I love mixing together old and new colourful items, combining Royal Danish porcelain, for example, with contemporary melamine tableware,' says Charlotte.

'My favourite colour changes often. My daughter often asks me what is your favourite colour this week?' *Charlotte Hedeman Gueniau*

Floors are wooden and neutral so the floral wallpapers and rugs can take centre stage.

A generous dining table includes cushions and napkins in floral designs, as well as real flowers.

Painted furniture in complementary colours picks up on the the pink roses in the kitchen.

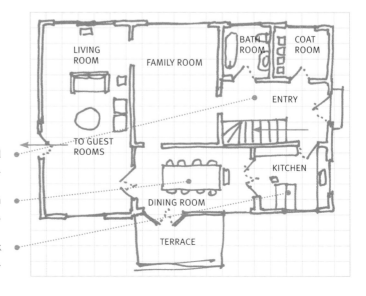

LOOKING ROSY
This page
Powerful floral wallpaper applied to the wall behind the sink and dishwasher is unexpected and delightfully bold, creating a joyous vibe in a room where flowers are never far from the surface.

PINK FIZZ
Opposite left
Floral fizzy pink wallpaper is a bold backdrop in the hallway, where painted wooden stools and crocheted cushions provide vivid complementary colours to the electric pink.

ROSES AND LIME *Opposite right* Papering only one wall in the kitchen leaves the rest of the space dedicated to displaying objects, china and lights in a vast array of bold and cheerful colours that dance against the vivid wall.

Floral Style Guidelines *Let flowers flourish in your space*

'If you have a lot of patterns, try to keep your palette simple. Too many prints are difficult to work with, if you also use different colours. It would be best to play with variations of the same colour.'

Madeline Weinrib, designer

1 INSPIRED BY FLOWERS
Take to the garden and look at the flowers you respond to the most. Shapes, form and colour will lead you towards what you love in decorating too.

2 PAPER THE WALLS
Wallpapers come in a variety of styles, from Art Deco cherry blossom designs that are as pretty as they are subtle, to glorious Technicolor mopheads and traditional country-style floral sprigs.

3 FURNITURE Try adding floral still lifes or motifs to the panels of a cupboard, or apply a delicate blossom or leaf motif to the sides or fronts of chests of drawers or chairs to personalize and stylize your own furniture.

4 FLORAL FABRICS
Pretty floral fabrics can be found from department stores to flea markets. Use them in unexpected places for a sense of surprise – on a mid-century chair or even to cover a padded door.

5 DECORATED CHINA
From Victorian era tea services to delicate Far Eastern porcelain tableware or 1960s graphic blooms, flowers are everywhere on china. Set the table with a plain white cloth and go floral with the place settings.

PATCHWORK POUFFE Stripes, checks, florals and plains all combine on this buttoned pouffe to provide colourful casual seating in Charlotte Hedeman Gueniau's home. Make your own version using fabric offcuts.

FLORAL TRIBUTE Painted flower panels on an oriental cupboard bring eastern exoticism to a Danish home. The cupboard provides decoration enough, when combined with a vase of flowers and a small painting.

'One thing to keep in mind is if you use a ton of bold patterns throughout your home, try to minimize clutter as the look can easily become a sensory overload. Pattern on pattern tends to work best in organized and chic spaces.' *Michelle Adams, designer*

6 HANDMADE FLOWERS
Get knitting or crocheting plate holders, placemats and plant pot covers using floral designs. Better still, create your own single flowers and use these as decoration.

7 HEIRLOOM QUILTS
Use vintage fabric or scraps of inherited floral fabric curtains to create quilts and throws that have personal meaning.

8 REAL FLOWERS
Use a variety of vintage vases in different colours and sizes. Pick wildflowers from the garden or make a bold graphic statement with a single bloom such as a camellia, hydrangea or sunflower.

9 FAKE FLOWERS
For year-round colour, keep a store of faux flowers that you bring out when the season is right. Combine some small orchids with a few larger blooms to be used as an informal arrangement on a windowsill.

10 ACCESSORIES
Lampshades can be covered with floral fabrics or plain ones embellished with 3D blooms. Add floral shaped door handles to chests of drawers. Or add a ceramic flower to the end of a light pull.

FLORAL CUISINE Have fun in the kitchen by collecting crocheted and embroidered pan coolers and display them with zingy tea towels. Flowers work well as a motif on all surfaces.

BOLD SPRIGS On a patchwork quilt, combine tiny spriggy florals with checks, stripes and a wide range of bold colours for a strong statement in a brightly coloured room.

Using Floral Fabrics

Whether on traditional curtains or contemporary upholstery, comfortable bedding or delicate cushions, floral fabrics are timeless and elegant.

1 Floral fabrics in unexpected places, such as these cushions on a mid-century armchair, make an unusual statement. Meanwhile a crocheted floral throw is a good way of continuing a floral theme in a subtle way.

2 Christina Strutt of Cabbages & Roses uses faded floral fabrics in delicate shades of buttercream and pale rose on many different surfaces including walls, curtains, throws and outdoor awnings.

3 Yvonne Eijkenduijn's Belgian living room comes with its own floral tribute and a sense of comfort, showing how white combines well with pink and red florals.

4 Vivid apple green provides a strong counterpoint to a combination of florals in this snug rustic bedroom belonging to Dutch designer Floriene Bosch.

5 In a modern take on traditional floral fabrics, classic chairs have been reupholstered in contemporary toile de Jouy designs and placed against a bold blue wall with flower paintings both old and new.

'Traditional floral fabrics have enduring appeal; the older and more faded they get the better. Buying fabrics for the home is a huge investment so it is important to use the most beautiful you can afford.'

Christina Strutt, designer

2

3

4

5

DINING STYLE Mid-century occasional chairs mingle with a swinging sixties dining table and upholstered chairs and a swirling blue bespoke rug in a dining room that offers comfort and welcome, and where the architectural merits of the space do not get lost in the mix.

'Jonny is the visionary behind the look of our groovy pad. When I come home I am happy to be surrounded by his colourful vision. It makes me smile.'

Simon Doonan

'The best rooms in a home are always comfy and optimistic.'

Jonathan Adler

ECLECTIC STYLE

Eclectic Style is all about mixing and matching, breaking rigid style rules and playing with colour to create something that is totally unique and inspiring.

Jonathan Adler, potter and interior designer, and Simon Doonan, writer and Creative Director of Barneys New York, have created an apartment in New York City that fits perfectly with their life. It is clear they had a ball creating their space. It has a vibrant luxury about it. Adler believes that a home should be all about beautiful, unimpeachable chic and full of gorgeous and well-designed objects.

In combining graphic patterns and bold colours, Adler and Doonan's cheerful apartment follows no set colour rules. 'We wanted to create a dreamy space so we painted everything – floors, ceilings and walls – bright white. Then we layered in lots of bold and colourful bits with wild abandon,' says Adler. 'We are very lucky to live in a large Manhattan apartment and find that we use every square inch. We bought a first apartment 14 years ago and the adjacent one six years ago.

HAPPY CHIC A symphony of bold colour, warm textures and lots of tempering white walls, the Adler–Doonan living room provides an inviting mix of mid-century furniture, vintage finds and contemporary ceramics. This is eclectic style at its very best.

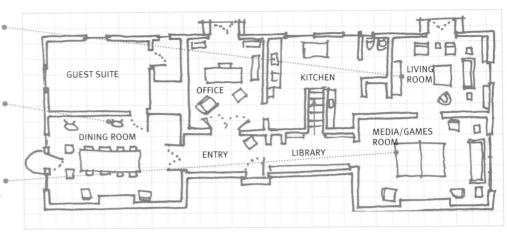

Large, bold rugs anchor the space in both living rooms.

Use mantels to display colourful collections of china or glass.

One living room was converted into a big dining room, the other became a comfortable seating space and a ping-pong room combined.

When we combined the apartments we struggled with what to do with the other living room. For a while we made it kind of formal and we never, ever used it and it was kinda' sad, just staring at us unused. That's when I decided to get rid of all the furniture and put a ping-pong table in the middle of the room and now we use it constantly.' Simon's most recent book was called *Eccentric Glamour* and that perfectly describes what he is looking for in interior and product design. 'I hate it when a house feels snobbish and designed to impress rather than be welcoming. So I strive to create stuff that is beautiful but has a dose of welcoming levity. The most successful aspect of our own personal design ethos is that it is a true reflection of who we are and it makes us happy every day. We like to call it happy chic.'

HAPPY FACES Witty ceramic objects and vases create a a still-life ensemble that will always elicit a positive response in any room.

'My favourite quote of all time is: Less is a bore.'

Jonathan Adler

GAME PLAN Two paintings by John-Paul Philippé depicting an abstract pair of eyes rest on the window mullions at the back of the living room and look over the ping-pong table. This space is smart and sophisticated but also effortlessly comfortable.

'If you can only afford one statement piece in a living room, make it an oversized chandelier. I think chandeliers should always be bigger than you think you need and more expensive than you think you can afford.'

Jonathan Adler

Eclectic Style Guidelines *Make your spaces fun and funky*

'Mix it up. If a room is too matchy-matchy, it'll look contrived. Instead, keep its colours and themes casually connected.' *Thom Filicia, designer*

1 CLASH MEANS CLASS
Throw out the colour rule book and mix up bold clashing colours and cheerful graphic patterns. Try deep browns and oranges, pastel blues and leaf greens, gold enamel and coloured glass.

2 GLASS ACT
Look out for vintage and mid-century glass vases, jugs and decorative pieces that work together. Range them across a windowsill so that natural light shines through them and casts a warming glow across a room.

3 PICK-AND-MIX FURNITURE
Eclectic means mismatching pieces that create their own cohesion. Look for furniture with metallic legs, 1960s style, to combine with eco pieces and some classic lighting.

4 ECLECTIC LIGHTING
Scour flea markets for floor-standing lights and table lamps. Combine the two and they will throw pools of light in the direction of your favourite pieces. Oversized Anglepoise lamps make a statement.

5 FINDING INSPIRATION
1950s advertising, magazines and books and design museums are all good sources for the eclectic feel. Flea markets and retro stores are great places for picking up one-off statement pieces.

QUIRKY CHIC This painting of 1960s singer Sly Stone by Ed Paschke provides a colourful backdrop for a navy blue velvet chair and zigzag rug, while salvaged wood is made chic with metal legs.

KINGS AND QUEENS Ceramics from Jonathan Adler's Utopia ceramic collection provide a witty way of displaying flowers that would work on a mantelpiece, tabletop or shelf.

'By masterfully mixing and layering collections of favourite objects and possessions you can create an enchanting, idiosyncratic mix that enhances the individuality of your space.' *Abigail Ahern, designer*

6 FOLLOW YOUR INSTINCT Creating an eclectic vibe is all about curating your belongings almost as though they were artefacts in an ever-changing museum. Play around by creating different configurations.

7 WALLS AND FLOORS Keeping floors and walls neutral gives you the freedom to create clashes of styles and colours elsewhere. Or, make them the focus of your eclecticism and experiment with bold wallpapers and fabrics.

8 FABRICS Adler and Doonan love geometrics and graphic devices and these can be found throughout the apartment. Strike a cohesive note using similar fabrics, colours or designs so there is a gentle coordination.

9 QUIRKY PIECES Making a statement is very much part of eclecticism. Display your favourite pieces in their best light by placing them prominently in a room or spotlighting them with LED floor or wall lights.

10 HUMOUR Eclectic often means witty and is a style that doesn't take itself too seriously. Go with your instinct when choosing the quirky and the downright wacky. If it makes you smile, buy it.

RETRO CORNER A smart seating area has been created beneath a statement piece of art by combining retro chairs with a glass-topped table and a metal sculptured base.

CUSTOMIZED CHIC A sleek, clean-lined cupboard has been rejuvenated by the addition of graphic floral fabric and chicken-wire panels. On top is a display of decorative ceramics that adds to the zing.

MODERN GLAMOUR STYLE

Modern Glamour is all about making a statement and preserving a sense of cool at the same time. Mix dramatic furniture with pale neutral colours, using glamorous materials such as velvet or marble in rooms with simple furniture layouts, or place unexpected pieces of furniture alongside one another to create an interesting rhythm.

In Orange County, Marc and Melissa Palazzo's home demonstrates perfectly how modern glamour is as much about personality and a bold commitment to mixing and matching as it is about off-the-shelf style. Chic but relaxed, the design duo, who run Pal + Smith in Newport Beach, describe their style as modern, eclectic, colourful and unexpected. 'We get our inspiration from fashion, old and new, vintage photography, Frida Kahlo paintings, old James Bond movies and Alfred Hitchcock. Often, we'll mix styles and genres, placing antiques next to vintage finds.'

'I love citrus colours,' says Melissa, 'and there is plenty of green and yellow throughout the house. Contrast is something we thrive on, whether in bold fabrics or paint. And statement chandeliers are another favourite device for introducing an element of surprise or drama.'

GLAMOROUS LIVING
Smart but friendly, the open-plan living area divides into an intimate 'grown up' area, a family area with a table and bookshelves and a relaxed sociable kitchen.

'I love to mix all styles.
I use a fair amount of
mid-century, Art Deco as
well as Asian antiques. I
think eclectic design is
the best. I want to keep
people guessing.'

Melissa Palazzo

DINING DELUXE In the dining room, colourful sheer curtains were added to soften the hard-edged glamour of a marble-topped dining table and functional dining chairs.

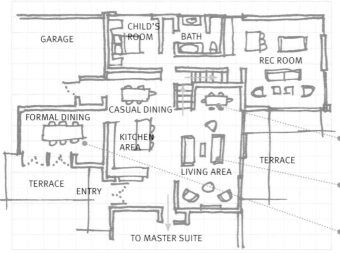

GARAGE

CHILD'S ROOM

BATH

REC ROOM

CASUAL DINING

FORMAL DINING

KITCHEN AREA

TERRACE

LIVING AREA

TERRACE

ENTRY

TO MASTER SUITE

The Palazzos use a bold mix of colours and textures, rather than a particular style, as a starting point in their designs. They also make full use of the indoor/outdoor style of the house, often throwing open the glass doors for entertaining or spilling the living space into an extended area outdoors. It makes for more relaxed and flexible living.

An elegant painted wooden table and low round stools give a hint of the boudoir at one end of the living space.

The living room features two Madison sofas from the collection of Pal + Smith that provide instant glamour in the open plan space.

Formal dining is at a marble-topped table flanked by leather chairs. Luxurious materials always denote glamour.

'Allow seriously grown-up wallpaper to take centre stage but not dominate a space. A mix of materials such as velvet, shiny wood and metal tones against a rich verdant green makes a striking combination in any space.'

Melissa Palazzo

MODERN ALCHEMY A luscious combination of forest green and blues plus a variety of textures lends unexpected glamour to a quiet seating area.

Modern Glamour Style Guidelines *Aim for elegance and eloquence*

'If you want a statement piece, it should be an expensive one, otherwise the statement you are making is "I can't afford anything better".' *Tom Delavan, designer*

MODERN MIX Work some glamour alchemy by mixing and matching different types of furniture for a modern feel. Try painted Asian-style tables alongside 1930s armoires or vintage French baroque furniture.

EVERYDAY DISGUISE Create instant drama and an element of surprise by using glamorous and diaphanous white or colourful curtains to conceal everyday clutter such as walk-in wardrobes or office paperwork.

CREATE CONTRAST Contrast rough with smooth, bold pattern with minimal floors and walls, colourful glass with neutral surfaces and the old with the new to create an interesting and unpredictable visual tension.

MIXING MATERIALS For a modern glamour masterclass gather together furniture that is a mix of glossy white, reflective steel, hard-edged but luxurious marble and in a range of decorative styles.

GLASS CLASS Tall vases and bottles in a variety of shapes and tones double-up as colour providers and smart display pieces. Place them on mantels, dining tables or consoles so their colour becomes an accent in a room.

TRUE BLUES A Nouveau ottoman from the Pal + Smith collection in jewel-bright turquoise fabric complements glass lights and objects, while a chunky display shelf echoes the espresso base of the box.

CLOSET ART An antique cupboard, one of Melissa Palazzo's favourite pieces in her home, makes a dramatic statement and doubles as a piece of art as well as a storage cupboard in the living space.

'Even if one is working within a budget, one custom piece in a sea of recognizable, mass-produced objects could be the *pièce de résistance* that suddenly turns a room from boring and predicable to innovative and sensational. I highly recommend it.' *Tori Mellott, style writer*

6 PICTURE PERFECT Use vintage drawings and colourful art to make a statement. Collect types of art that are personal to you, such as animal images, favourite landscapes or family portraits.

7 SMART TEXTILES Luxury means deliciously tactile textiles. Think of rich velvet or chenille used in combination with damask or textured linens in bold colours, graphic patterns or stylized floral designs.

8 CHIC WALLPAPER Wallpaper always adds glamour and visual interest to a space. Keep it confined to one wall or one part of a room for the most impact. Bold patterns or motifs in muted colours provides a smart backdrop.

9 LIGHTING TRICKS, Mid-century modern floor lamps, 19th-century chandeliers and cool contemporary Italian globe lights all add to the glamour story. Don't be shy about including a big light in every room for instant impact.

10 COCOONING From suspended cocoon bamboo chairs to oversized sofas upholstered in bold and glamorous patterns, modern glamour is about creating smart, effortless comfort.

DELICATE GLAMOUR For a smart still life on a marble dining table surface group delicate glass decanters in signature shades of citrus, burnt orange and turquoise to create a little luxury.

RELAXED DINING In spare space beneath the stairs, a curious mix of Asian art, feminine stools and a traditional table make an understated but undeniably glamorous area in which to work.

"Your home should tell the **story** of who you are, and be a collection of what you LOVE brought together under one roof."

Nate Berkus

Room by Room

EASY ENTERTAINING
Previous page In Christine
d'Ornano's London kitchen
a generous-sized reclaimed
refectory table and a set of
colourful retro dining chairs
look elegant combined with
overhead utility lamps.

'Think twice before incorporating a trend concept or material into the kitchen. In fact, the more rewarding road to a truly lasting kitchen design is to define your very own personal style.'

Susan Serra, kitchen designer

UTILITARIAN CHIC *This page*
Mixing vintage accessories and retro wall tiles with industrial style cabinets and bar stools, this kitchen is both functional and easy on the eye. Design-wise, it is easy to move from one sphere of activity to another.

KITCHENS

At the core of every happy home is a kitchen. Whether large or small, smart or informal, cosy or minimal, it is the kitchen in which friends and family gather, and where cooking, eating and entertaining take place. You can indulge your decorating passion by planning a layout that suits both the way you live and the things you love. The best kitchens are those that combine function, personality and good design, spaces where you want to both linger and also feel a sense of purpose.

Start to think about what your priorities should be. Do you have an empty space to plan or, more likely, are you looking to remodel or revamp? Look at as many different types of kitchens and layouts as possible. Make a floor plan of your space and play around with different configurations on paper before gathering in quotations from kitchen designers.

KITCHEN DESIGN is all about fitting what you need into the space you have available. Small kitchens often call for single-run galley arrangements or a compact L-shaped configuration, while larger spaces can often accommodate island units, U-shaped layouts and different zones of activity. Planning at an early stage is important, whether you are reconfiguring or starting from scratch.

The work triangle This classic idea dictates that the three main areas of cooking activity, namely the sink, the cooker and the fridge, should form a loose triangle so that you can move from one to another in the most efficient way. This isn't always possible, but it makes sense to store everyday tableware close to the dishwasher and for cooking equipment to be kept close to the oven, for example, to save on time and energy.

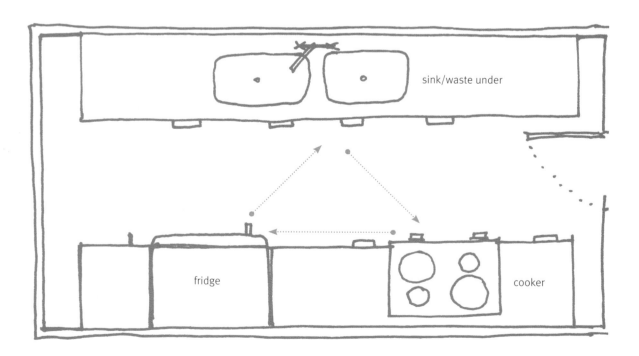

sink/waste under

fridge

cooker

CLEAN-LINED KITCHEN *Opposite* In a converted ground floor kitchen Sania Pell opened out one wall as a window to the garden so that the dining table could take centre stage in a room that marries function with understated style.

'A kitchen has to be pretty. That's important to me, but even more important is that it has to be functional, well thought out and carefully designed.'

Fernanda Bourlot,
designer

Kitchen Layouts

Work out your personal priorities, then plan your space around them

Kitchen design is dependent on the space available, how many people will use it and whether it is purely a cooking space or also doubles up as an eating and/or living area. Gather tear sheets of kitchen elements you love and use them to build up a picture of your dream kitchen.

'I love to mix new Scandinavian design with old Scandinavian, French and English farm antiques. I do not like fancy antiques. I like simplicity and functionality in furniture.'

Yvonne Eijkenduijn, blogger

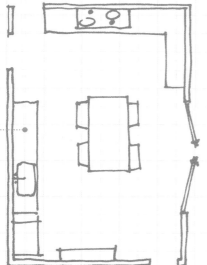

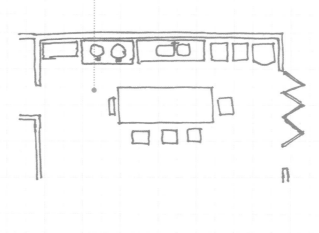

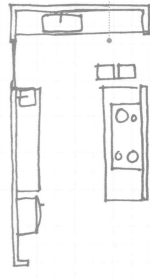

LOOSE L-SHAPED *Opposite* A loose L-shaped layout works well in a kitchen that is large enough for a dining table and distinct areas for cooking and food preparation. The tall walls have been used to house generous glass-fronted cupboards to display attractive items such as food containers and books, while undercounter cupboards contain cooking equipment.

ISLAND RETRO *Above left* In a ground floor space a single run of units and appliances that includes a sink, an Aga cooker and a fridge is balanced by a freestanding island unit that doubles up as a food preparation and eating area. Single-run kitchens are suitable for small spaces, where they also need wall cupboards to provide storage.

DOUBLE GALLEY *Above right* In a long rectangular room a double galley layout makes for a functional food preparation space. Here a third wall has been used to provide a sink and a more generous run of worktop space plus additional storage in open pigeon-holes on the wall. Serious cooks keep paraphernalia to hand; utensils are ranged across a rail above the worktop.

Kitchens: Planning

The fun starts when you draw up a plan

GETTING THE ESSENTIALS RIGHT

Your choice of materials will depend on what decorative approach you choose. There are many decisions to make but here are the basics to help you pick on a look.

You will always need some cupboards so decide what it is you really love: wood or painted, matt or gloss, fitted or unfitted.

Worktops are important. Spend money on the best surface you can afford – corian, slate, steel or zinc – wood for tough, hardwearing surfaces, or laminates if your budget is tight.

Flooring has to be tough and easy to clean, so think about ceramic tiles, flagstones, vinyl or linoleum, cork, slate or painted concrete.

Walls in work areas can benefit from tiling or panelling in glass or steel. If left plain, remember to paint them with mould-resistant kitchen paint.

Lighting should be varied, with LED spots placed under wall cupboards for lighting work surfaces and overall dimmers so you can adjust light levels at different times of the day.

Keep window coverings minimal and useful. Fabric and wooden blinds work best, but if you love colour introduce some floral fabrics or pattern on cushion textiles or tea towels, or incorporate them in cupboard panels.

The best kitchens are those that work on a functional and aesthetic level. Before you start thinking about replacing a kitchen or planning a new one from scratch, take some time to think about what it is you need. Are you a keen cook who prepares fresh meals every day for yourself and/or a family? Do you like to cook alone or is it more likely that two people will be working in the space on a regular basis? Are you a tidy person who likes to have everything hidden away in dust-free cupboards or do you like to see tableware and your *batterie de cuisine* on display and at the ready?

Do the tear-sheet trick and pick out images of kitchens you are emotionally drawn to. It may be materials, colour, large windows, great flooring or fantastic tiles that take your fancy. Or you may find yourself returning to a perfectly white and wood space, where everything feels fresh but serene.

Your type of space will often push your design in a certain direction. A small space with tall ceilings may call for incorporating split-level areas or mezzanines in order to create a room within a room. A larger space allows you to spread your design wings and add in big one-off pieces of vintage cook's furniture such as a butcher's block or a rough-hewn dining table that's seen a lot of life. In a bigger space you have more layout options and the walls and floors have an opportunity to take centre stage.

SINK CHIC *Above and opposite* In this Brooklyn home a reclaimed sink inspired the design of a simple white and wood kitchen that takes its design cue from natural materials: slate, wood, ironwork and steel all working together in a happy harmony of new and reclaimed elements.

'Think of a kitchen as a machine.'

Fitzhugh Karol, designer

Storage on Display *Make a feature of favourite objects and display them for all to see*

In the kitchen there are always plenty of opportunities to create some interesting eye candy from everyday items. In a cook's kitchen it may be shiny utensils suspended from hanging racks or rails. Colourful china may dominate a lively family kitchen or a serial collector may have an entire tableware collection that needs to be seen rather than hidden away in a dusty cupboard.

Hanging rails are a great device to have around the cooking area, either positioned above the hob on a tiled surface or at the side of a range cooker or food preparation area. If you have an island unit then create a hanging system above it by installing a dedicated rack from the ceiling. A freestanding butcher's block placed up against a wall looks good with a

hanging rail above it on which butcher's hooks can be used to display anything from a row of decorative jugs to china cups.

Open display units may take the form of pigeon-hole shelving, either freestanding or attached to a wall, or else a unit with shelving in which displayed objects take centre stage.

COOK'S CORNER *Above* A neat storage unit houses deep drawers for plenty of cooking equipment in this well-stocked kitchen. Pans that are used every day hang happily from a chrome rail placed beneath the cooker hood.

ELEGANT DISPLAY *Above* A simple wooden display unit backed with reclaimed timber forms the perfect textured backdrop for a collection of everyday glassware and ceramics in this Danish kitchen. Practical storage and delicious display rolled into one.

'If possible, for a dramatic, new look, paint the cabinets. A sophisticated off-white, in a sort of mushroom, light khaki shade is easy to live with, classic and elegant.' *Susan Serra, kitchen designer*

It makes sense to store and display everyday china and glassware so it's at hand and place seldom used but pleasing platters or soup tureens higher up the display ladder.

When storing china, group it according to colour or style for more impact and make sure that any really precious pieces are stored in such a way that they're not easy to knock over. Glazed cupboards, either wall-mounted or undercounter, are a good way to protect china from breakages and the accumulation of grime and dust open shelving acquires over time. They can be transparent, opaque or frosted depending on how much visibility you are after.

CONCRETE IDEA *Above* Concrete block shelves attached to the wall by strong steel supports provide a stone-like tableau for a display of everyday ceramics and fern-like plants.

CUPBOARD LOVE *Above* A classic collection of blue and white china together with glasses and coffee cups and saucers looks informally at home in a glazed wall cupboard, which is perfect for keeping ceramics free from dust but on display.

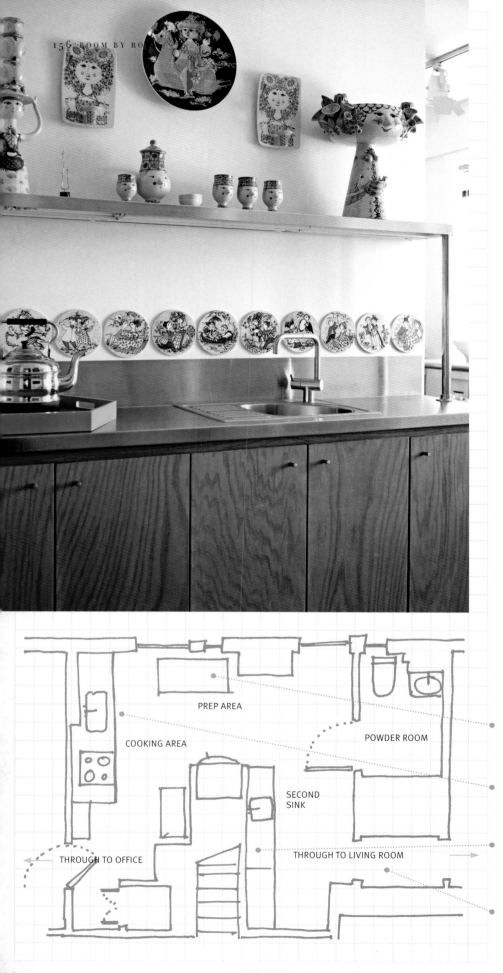

PREP AREA

COOKING AREA

POWDER ROOM

SECOND
SINK

THROUGH TO OFFICE ←

THROUGH TO LIVING ROOM →

In Manhattan Jonathan Adler and Simon Doonan's kitchen combines sleek functionalism with groovy displays of quirky ceramic jugs and vases to create a cooking space that brims with personality and panache. A mix of materials echoes perfectly the colours of the assembled ceramics on a purpose-built steel shelf. The kitchen slips neatly into an L-shaped space to one end of the apartment and combines bespoke units and fixtures alongside a built-in original glass-fronted cupboard used for storage. Adler's ceramic collection is beautifully showcased along shallow steel shelving placed above the work areas at eye level to provide a visual treat while cooking or preparing food.

Plates mounted just above the stainless steel splashback make for a witty way of complementing the repetitive task of doing the dishes. Flush-fitted plain wooden cupboards are practical as their smooth lines are easy to keep clean. Neat, tiny door knobs work well for the same reason.

CHINA DOLLS *Left* Intricate china figurines and plates, some by ceramic artist Bjorn Wiinblad, add a quirky and colourful touch to the sleek industrial-style kitchen sink.

CERAMICS ON PARADE *Opposite* Work with any existing built-in cupboards and butt new units up to them for a mix and match finish. Or incorporate a larder-style cupboard in a different design and finish to create the same effect.

Conventional fitted units combine with freestanding storage trolleys and built-in original cupboards.

Plenty of undercounter storage means there is space left over for display shelves.

Soften industrial-style fittings with displays of china and tableware.

Slate floors are a sensible idea for homes with pets. They are easy to care for and easy to clean.

'A feeling of eccentric glamour and irreverent luxury perfectly describes what I try to create in interior and product design.' *Jonathan Adler*

URBAN KITCHEN

In city apartments where space is usually limited, it is often best to design a kitchen that is simple and functional so that you can add personality in the details. Let the materials take centre stage: stainless steel, wood and slate are all pleasing solutions that work well together or on their own. Add in detailing by displaying china or ceramics, or make a feature of shiny cooking equipment.

'Repaint the back wall and/or side walls of glass-door cabinets. Adding a fresh colour of raspberry, coral or an elegant charcoal colour against white dishes will dramatically change the look.' *Susan Serra, kitchen designer*

HANDMADE CUPBOARD In Alayne Patrick's Brooklyn apartment a sink storage unit has been built using vintage cupboard doors and handles, while open pigeon-holes on the wall provide storage and display space for an eclectic china and glass collection.

Built-in Storage *Out of the way but not out of view*

When you are redesigning or reconfiguring a kitchen, built-in storage is one of the most important aspects of making sure you can fit all your equipment into your space. Take a look around at the huge variety of cupboard styles that are available and remember to think about handles and door knobs at the same time.

It can be tempting to follow kitchen manufacturers' advice and kit out your room with as many cupboards that you can cram into the space. More important though is to make an inventory of all your kitchen equipment. There will always be some redundant pieces you can edit out. Next, work out which items will look good on display, which ones you need to have for everyday use and those that are best hidden way. Then you can calculate how many cupboards you will need and which ones can double up as display units. It's good to aim to have some built-in units, as these are the engine room of any storage scheme, whether they are discreet, plain-door affairs or bold glossy design statements.

WHITE STYLE *Above* Amy Neunsinger's kitchen includes simply styled white cupboards and drawers that are completed with mesh panelling, retro steel handles and glass knobs.

ELECTRIC ECLECTIC *Above* Bright and cheerful ceramics sit in glazed cabinets next to an open display of ceramic designer Jonathan Adler's deliciously original collection.

CASE STUDY

COOK'S KITCHEN

A kitchen in which cooking is the main focus calls for a happy mix of function and creativity. More often than not a cook's kitchen includes some form of island or breakfast bar. Serious cooks spend a lot of time in this room, so they prefer to create a working space where friends and family can also gather round the food preparation area to talk, help or watch.

Amy Neunsinger's splendid Los Angeles kitchen showcases the best of vintage utility with a classic island layout that enables efficient movement throughout the space. Worktops are sleek marble, while at the heart of the space a stunning generous sink designed by Michael S. Smith for Kallista is both a focal point and functional. The cooking and food preparation activity can be flexible thanks to the inclusion of two sinks. One is a focal point for the room and is at the head of the island unit.

UTILITY CHIC Industrial materials and a white-and-steel colour theme create a glamorous, hardworking foodie workspace where exposed pipework and luxurious surfaces mingle well to create a smart utility vibe.

'I wanted that "old with the new" here. I love that feeling where you get those old materials and that mingling of the indoor and the outdoor too.' *Amy Neunsinger*

To soften the hard surfaces of concrete on the floor and marble on the worktops, lighter touches have been added in the form of flowers, opalescent tiles beneath the sink and appealing vintage taps and accessories, as well as utility-style door knobs and handles.

White custom-made wooden units inlaid with wire mesh panels mix well with open shelving that displays and stores glassware and tableware. Having everyday china on display is a great way to minimize work in the kitchen, especially when the dishwasher is only a step away in the island unit.

Wall-mounted glass-fronted cupboards are used for storing cookery books and cooking equipment and are designed to look as though they are part of the original fixtures and fittings. A big bold fridge is in keeping with the industrial-style range cooker on the other side of the island.

THEATRICAL SINK *Left* Food preparation is never a chore when you have a deliciously generous sink and a serious tap and plate rinser. Work takes centre stage at this solid island unit.

WHITE ON WHITE *Opposite* Sleek glass splashbacks reflect the natural outdoor light onto white Thassos marble worktops, both from Walker Zanger, while vintage-style taps lend retro glamour to a functional workspace.

THROUGH TO FAMILY ROOM

KITCHEN AREA

TERRACE

THROUGH TO LIVING ROOM

THROUGH TO GARDEN ROOM

The classic triangle of sink, fridge and cooker are in a straight line here to minimize time spent circling the island unit.

Allow enough space around an island unit for traffic flow.

Keep the activity centre of the kitchen away from French doors where access is required at all times of the day.

Make good use of tall ceilings by installing tall cupboards and shelving.

'Open shelving is great for easy access, but it's also nice to view my pottery.' *Amy Neunsinger*

Casual Eating *Sharing a meal with family and friends is one of life's great joys*

The days of formal dining are no longer with us, mainly because the idea of a separate dining room, for best only, is no longer considered to be an important element of many homes. In its place, the kitchen has become a central space, where the daily activities of cooking, eating and relaxing are more likely to take place in the same area rather than in separate rooms.

Although formality may not be key, there are many ways to make a dining experience feel special for your guests or family. Rather than formal table settings, a starchy white tablecloth and a 'best' dinner service, make the space comfortable and welcoming with subtle lighting, a friendly table covering, whether it be cotton, linen or plastic, mismatching china and everyday rather than heirloom cutlery. That way you keep the dining experience real, relaxing and inviting.

SETTING THE SCENE

Source a dining table that provides some flexibility. Having either an extendable or folding one allows you to cater easily for unexpected or extra guests.

Chairs are important. The more comfortable the better, although if space is tight folding ones make sense.

Chair cushions will add to the comfort factor and may be covered in matching or complementary colours to the rest of the space.

Start a tablecloth collection: a waxed oilcloth for everyday and family use; crisp Egyptian cotton for the perfect backdrop to colourful tableware and china.

Include candles, and plenty of them, either in the form of discreet tea lights or a couple of candelabra for romantic moments.

COUNTRY IN THE CITY *Above* A pretty tablecloth and simple china against fuchsia pink chair cushions and a painted floor is understated yet supremely enticing in a kitchen/diner. A vintage china collection sits happily on simple wooden shelving that is painted white to allow its display of tableware to shine.

'A laid-back, relaxed home comes from allowing real life to be a part of your design mixing old with new, luxurious with everyday and family heirlooms with kids' paintings, where the odd imperfection is celebrated and friends and family can come together and not worry about "messing up" the interior decor!'

Atlanta Bartlett, designer

UNDERSTATED ELEGANCE In Anna-Malin Lindgren's Swedish home a gateleg table is extended when guests are expected. By day the table is used for crafting, but during the evening garden flowers and butterfly glass decorations set the scene for dinner with friends. Mismatching cane and metal chairs create an air of informality.

ZINC ALLURE A vintage zinc table is a surprising but effective choice in this Copenhagen dining room, where guests get a good view of the fascinating china collection.

'Watch the clutter! Few, quality, decorative additions to the kitchen present a more simple, yet elegant, appearance than too many. Take a second look, too, at your things that "live" on the counter. Less really is more!'

Susan Serra, kitchen designer

'Friends relax in my kitchen to enjoy a drink and appetizers while I cook. Comfortable seating and an island to prepare food so that they can watch while I'm cooking were essential.'

Fernanda Bourlot, designer

DINER STYLE Tucked into a corner of a kitchen are two small open shelving units arranged to form an impromptu eating and gathering area. Bar chairs encourage guests to stop and linger.

'I like our home because in it we have created an airy environment that is conducive both to a big family and to entertaining.' *Melissa Palazzo*

ISLAND QUEEN *Above* A super-sleek island in white wood and with a chunky zinc worktop reigns supreme without dominating this casual, functional kitchen space. It is deep enough to provide seating and plenty of storage.

ROOM WITH A VIEW *Opposite* At first glance you would never know a kitchen area is incorporated into this open-plan ground floor living space. White walls and floors pave the way for a brown, steel and citrus green colour scheme that helps to disguise the kitchen area.

SOCIABLE KITCHEN

When kitchens are integral to either a living or dining space the best decorating trick is to allow them to meld into the room as a sociable space rather than making too much of a statement with them. Units can be painted to blend in with the walls and ceiling, while jolts of accent colours can be picked out in both the living area and the kitchen to unify the space. Keeping the tiles or other splashback the same colour as the walls also helps with this process.

This kitchen forms part of a well-considered open-plan living space that has been opened out in all directions to create interesting zone of activity, that each work really well. It belongs to Marc and Melissa Palazzo of Pal + Smith, who have managed to create a neat kitchen space at one end of the room where all the functional elements are tucked away down one side. The kitchen is generous in size but in no way eats into or impedes the living space. A deep island unit doubles as a breakfast bar and storage space, as well as a space divider.

'Antiques and vintage play a big part in getting modern glamour right in an entertaining space.'

Melissa Palazzo

Seating at the island unit is complemented by a dining table and chairs a few steps away so entertaining is made super easy, with guests able to move smoothly from the living space to a natural conversation area centred around the island while the cook is busy and then on to the dining table to eat.

From the living space all you see of the kitchen area is a wall opening with a vista through to the dining space and neat, chunky shelving that displays everyday china. A smooth stainless steel fridge reflects great natural light back into the living space and so becomes barely noticeable. Dark wooden plinths help to echo the dark wood elsewhere in the ground floor, on ceiling beams, upholstery and the staircase.

So that the kitchen area can be quite contained, there are further deep storage units and wall-mounted cupboards with frosted panelling fitted to the side wall in the dining space. A fantastic focal point is provided by the gnarled wooden dining table and retro dining chairs that dominate the eating area.

Laying a concrete floor throughout the ground floor is a good way of anchoring each zone within the same shared space, while an animal-skin rug in the living area helps to delineate the relaxing area.

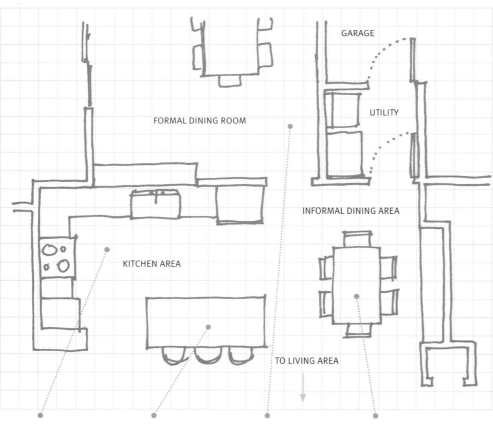

GARAGE

FORMAL DINING ROOM

UTILITY

INFORMAL DINING AREA

KITCHEN AREA

TO LIVING AREA

Cooker, sink and dishwasher are tucked away so they are hidden from view in the rest of the living area.

A discreet, functional island provides storage and seating space.

A more formal dining room is situated beyond, with easy access to the kitchen area through the opening in the wall.

Close to the kitchen space is a dining table for informal entertaining and family suppers.

'I designed this organic table as a cornerstone for the space.'

Melissa Palazzo

DINE IN STYLE The table is king in this cool dining space with its mismatched retro-inspired chairs and plenty of built-in storage. Lighting is provided by an overhead pendant, bespoke wall lights and built-in spotlights within the units for maximum flexibility.

LIVING SPACES

More than any other room your living space is your nest, your sanctuary and the one space that should reflect you to the core. Whether you love colour or country style, retro informality or modern glamour, your living space gives you the chance to kick back and relax with family and friends or even on your own, for a spot of 'me' time.

However you choose to decorate the space make sure it works for you, as a reflection of your personality and preferences as well as a space in which there are no distractions to stop you relaxing. If you have small children you may want to save serious investment in new furniture for later and instead make sure you have a couple of sets of washable covers for now. Tools such as colour, pattern and fabrics are good temporary measures for shifting the look of a living space.

LIVING SPACE DESIGN calls for thought about your furniture. Do you need to incorporate all your existing sofas and chairs or can you ditch dreary specimens and invest in a designer piece, a retro sofa or simply a smart new contemporary chair to liven up what you already have? Storage, coffee tables and how to incorporate home entertainment are other key things to consider.

Working around a rectangle Think about your furniture layout in any living space. Create a seating area around a focal point such as a fireplace, a large coffee table and rug or to one side of a room divider. You can vary the shape by placing individual chairs at an angle or by using an L-shaped sofa, drawing furniture in or out if space allows.

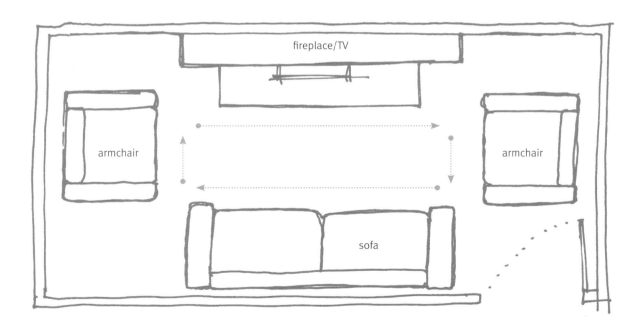

fireplace/TV

armchair

armchair

sofa

COMFORT AND JOY *Opposite* The smart combination of animal skins for warmth and texture, a comfortable white sofa set against wide zinc tables, the clean lines of metal window frames and the huge amounts of natural light is one that generates a simple welcome in Amy Neunsinger's Los Angeles home.

'With custom and made-to-order a person can tackle the challenges of an awkward space, a secondary problem such as storage or the problem of colour. If money is no object, a person can get precisely what they want without ever having to compromise and that is the ultimate luxury.' *Tori Mellott, style writer*

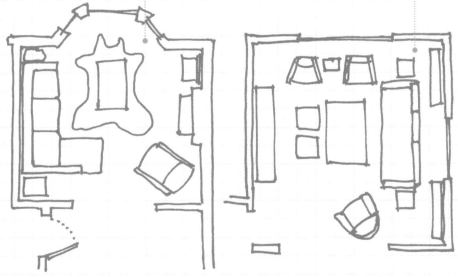

L-SHAPED LIVING *Above left* An L-shaped sofa helps to make a cosy seating area. A single chair placed diagonally next to the focal point of the fireplace further encloses the space. An animal-skin rug underneath the rectangular coffee table helps to break up the straight lines of the sofa and furniture and create an additional focal point in the centre.

U-SHAPED COLOUR *Above right* In a square living space, a central U-shaped furniture configuration will form an intimate seating area around a central focal point. A sofa flanked by chairs offers the most versatile arrangement for seating. Coffee tables work well as focal points and here a marble table creates a neutral focus among a sea of colour.

FURNITURE RULES *Opposite* Sometimes the furniture itself can act as a focal point. In a space with relatively little furniture, two black contemporary sofas become the main visual focus in a converted industrial building that is painted white throughout. A white rug softens the concrete floor but does not provide visual distraction from the sofas.

Living Space Layouts

Develop some harmony, balance and colour in your living space

Making a room feel comfortable is about bringing together a number of different elements that work with each other. Furniture placement, scale, balance, colour and furnishings are all important starting points before you decide which design direction you wish to go in. So kick off your shoes, relax and start playing around with some ideas on graph paper.

'Living rooms are social spaces, so hide your television and make sure to have at least three seating positions: a sofa and two others.'

Maxwell Gillingham-Ryan, interior designer/blogger

MID-CENTURY MODERN LIVING

Creating a living room with mid-century furniture is all about understatement and clean lines, while allowing graphic patterns and motifs to provide the decoration.

Virginia Armstrong of Roddy & Ginger set about making her minimal but comfortable living space to be a relaxing and clear space with no unnecessary adornment to complicate the atmosphere. This style of living room works well in small spaces and rooms where one existing focal point such as a neat fireplace or a feature wall with floor to ceiling windows or exposed brickwork takes the most visual focus.

CLEAN LINES LIVING
Simple but inviting, this light-filled living space has nothing that is not beautiful within its walls. It is a calming space in which you cannot fail to feel a sense of repose. The perfect place for relaxing after a busy day.

'I love collecting but hate clutter, so it's always a challenge to create a balance between a clean, calm living space and my obsession with boot sales and flea markets.' *Virginia Armstrong*

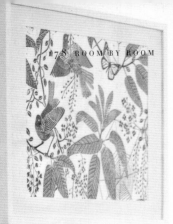

'As a textile designer I am in love with colour and pattern, and how it can add warmth and personality to a simple space.'

Virginia Armstrong

By placing the decorative emphasis on colour and texture, it is a gentle layering of materials that produces these comfortable results. Armstrong, a textile designer, has created a clever combination of zesty blues and greens, accent fabrics and designs to complement natural autumnal tones in the room, on the wooden floor and wood-framed furniture, in the artwork and on the sofa cushions. A woollen rug topped with a ropework pouffe provides welcome warmth.

Confronted with a simple space and a wooden floor, it is often easier to fill the space with much furniture and a riot of colour and objects, but here a few carefully considered pieces of furniture are elegant individual pieces that are curated well together to form a nod to mid-century design without slavishly following the look, as though from a design history manual. The walls are kept plain apart from a handful of images that are a mixture of vintage finds and Armstrong's own graphic designs.

AUTUMN SHADES *Opposite* Combining forest browns with leaf greens then adding in a warm turquoise to the mix creates a warming palette in a room where plain comfort is the key look. Browns work best when they are used in a careful balance with lighter, brighter colours.

DANISH COMFORT *Right* A Danish modern easy chair is lined with a sheepskin rug to make a warm retreat next to the picture window and below a quirky display shelf where disparate objects form a happy display of personally collected items.

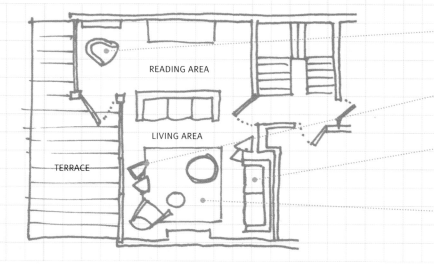

READING AREA

LIVING AREA

TERRACE

Always include a single chair in the seating scheme, even if you have two sofas.

Nests of tables are a flexible choice for occasional surfaces in a living space.

Two sofas enclose the living space with one of them forming a space divider.

On wooden floors use rugs to define and warm the space.

SMART ELEGANCE *Above left*
Sofas with stylized legs are particularly elegant for small spaces. They appear to take up less space when you can see air underneath them.

VINTAGE COMFORT *Above right*
A traditional sofa mixed with a vintage lamp and contemporary shelves is a good example of mixing and matching eras and styles to create a stylish room.

CONTEMPORARY LEATHER
Below Warm up leather seating with sheepskin and interesting textures. Here a glamorous gold lamé cushion provides a jolt of reflective colour.

PERFECT PAIR *Opposite* This pair of 1950s easy chairs upholstered in cappuccino colours are elegant additions to a period marble and plaster fireside, bringing comfort and colour.

Seating for Living Spaces

Think about seating as a decorating tool as well as a functional item

With thousands of sofa and chair styles and materials available, only your imagination limits the potential of transforming a room using only seating, taking fabric and cushions as your guide.

'The true beauty of a room can be found in its details. Layering a room with the items you love elevates your space.'

Nate Berkus, designer

'The crucial elements for relaxed spaces are lighting and seating – pretty much everything else works to flavour the experience. Upholstery has to work harder than most furniture – it needs to be sublimely comfortable, and at the same time it has to look sublime and inviting to get you to sit in it. ' *Russell Pinch, furniture designer*

SEATING AS DECORATION

Chairs make great statement pieces, carrying a confident swagger with their design credentials on their sleeve.

If you cannot afford a design classic original, save up for a reproduction piece. Many 1950s and 1960s classics are being reproduced at a lower cost than collector's auctions will throw up.

Comfort should take priority over style when it comes to key seating pieces, but add a touch of quirky invention when you get to choose occasional chairs or sofas.

If you have a favourite chair or sofa, allow it to influence the overall look of a space, whether its leather material calls for a masculine, modern approach, a wooden-framed sofa means that a Danish modern look beckons or a squashy sofa means that country comfort becomes the only option.

Sometimes a room needs a chair as a finishing touch once everything else is in place. Now's the time to search the internet or flea markets for a signature chair that can be reupholstered, restored or repainted to round off your scheme.

Don't forget the detailing. Piping, cushions, bolsters and throws all add definition, colour, comfort and glamour to your favourite seating choices.

Cushions can be as simple as fabric squares or as complex as hand-embroidered creations or tapestry blocks. Enjoy seeking out ones you love and set aside some time to make up your own designs and creations.

FORMAL ARMCHAIR *Above*
This black leather armchair combines high style with supreme comfort. It acts as a visual anchor near the casually displayed artworks.

SEVENTIES GLAMOUR *Below*
The Chippendale Arm Chair by Jonathan Adler is painted a complementary orange while his Mod Model cushion ties the decoration to a 1970s vibe.

SIMPLY WHITE *Above* Proving that white need not mean cool, this modern but comfortable sofa is warmed up with a woollen throw and handmade cushions in complementary neutral colours.

DISCREET NEUTRALITY *Below* Sometimes sofas are best left to recede into a room in which other elements – ceramics, artwork, rugs and furniture – make a decorative statement.

FLORAL CORNER *Above* Use unexpected fabric to update a retro find. This mid-century armchair has been given a facelift with a floral fabric to create an inviting easy chair.

COOL CORNER *Below* In a room full of colourful items and neutral walls this upholstered armchair with a statement cushion brings all the comfort of woven wool and tradition to a quiet corner.

COLOUR CODA Christine d'Ornano has developed an innate sense of colour from her many travels throughout the USA, Mexico and France. Every room in the house displays a sensitive use of colour.

RELAXED LUXURY

Setting aside a space in your home for informal entertaining is one of life's great pleasures. Either incorporate a dining table into an existing space such as a kitchen or living room, or, if space permits, create a dining room that is not so much a formal entertaining space but one that is comfortable and creative, or a room where different activities can take place during the day but at night the table can be laid for guests, whether unexpected or planned.

Christine d'Ornano, International Vice President of cosmetic company Sisley, and her financier husband, Marzouk Al-Bader, have enjoyed converting their Kensington home from a series of negelected and rundown apartments. Opposite their living room, they have successfully created a multipurpose room that is part dining room, part library, part homework space for their three children and part cosy relaxing space away from the formal living room. It is all effortlessly elegant. Huge doors padded with sapphire blue velvet and brass studs elevate the space to one of slight opulence. Within are reproduction Louis XVI-style chairs upholstered in yellow leather. 'I knew I wanted yellow chairs,' explains Christine, 'while for my husband comfort was a top priority, so this is a good example of our decorating team work.'

CORNER SPOT Relaxed comfort is a key element in this Kensington house. A retro side table lends glamour to a traditional and comfortable sofa placed near the window to catch the sunshine in daylight.

Unlike many Kensington residents they did not employ a designer to help them with their design decisions. Christine and her husband enjoy working together when it comes to decoration. 'Marzouk has a good eye. It was he who chose the lacquer grey colour for the front living room walls, while I picked out some pink linen for the sofa area. We make joint decisions when buying furniture and don't often have any decorating disasters.'

The living room is artfully arranged, with a comfortable mix of old and new furniture, contemporary art and objects. On the walls hang pieces of contemporary art by Gary Hume and Tracey Emin, while the seating includes a white Joe Colombo chair and a red Gerrit Rietveld piece that sit either side of an André Dubreuil stool with a tapestry seat stitched by Christine's mother Isabelle.

ELEGANT DINING *Left* Round tables are good for informal entertaining and for creating a relaxed intimacy for small family gatherings. Books are easily to hand in this dining space that doubles as a family library.

COMFORTABLE SEATING *Opposite* The living room includes plenty of seating as it is where visitors gather. 'The small Lalanne crocodile chairs are used only when we have a lot of people over and run out of seats,' says Christine.

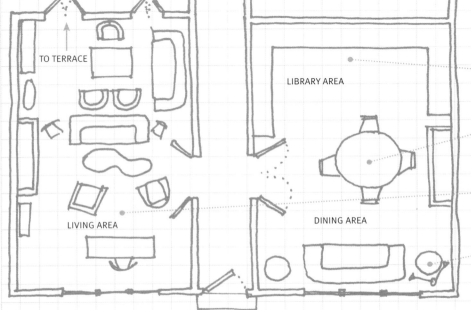

TO TERRACE

LIBRARY AREA

LIVING AREA

DINING AREA

Open shelving is used for displaying books while cupboards beneath store children's craft materials and tableware.

A circular table saves on space and creates an intimate, informal dining area at the centre of the room.

Double doors mirror the living space and library/dining room, with a comfortable seating area visible from the dining table.

Retro furniture provides glamour and mixes well with a traditional sofa and a more contemporary table.

'We make joint
decisions when
buying furniture.
If one of us really
dislikes a piece then
we won't buy it,
but often our tastes
coincide.'

Christine d'Ornano

Outdoor Living *Extend living space outdoors and decorate it with relaxation in mind*

Creating an outdoor room is a good way of creating additional living space when you cannot expand your home. It can be as simple as a decked area for an outdoor eating space or as complex as a multi-level seating and entertaining area.

Think about your climate and what you can realistically include in any outdoor scheme. Soft furnishings in the form of movable cushions work in both hot and colder climates as they can be moved indoors when the weather turns. Make sure wooden furniture is treated to protect it from damp conditions.

'For instant impact on a limited budget, try to keep all the fabrics coordinated with a simple colour scheme. Pick a basic background colour and two accent colours and try to stick within those colours.' *Celerie Kemble, designer*

Lighting can take the form of fixed spots in decking and steps or temporary decorative strings brought out for summer or special parties. Have fun with decorative features and experiment with colours that suit your planting scheme.

TROPICAL RETREAT *Above left* In an Orange County garden a bamboo-lined seating area is made cosy with wooden low-level loungers furnished with generous cushions in verdant greens.

MEDITERRANEAN DECKING *Above right* Taking inspiration from the Mediterranean, this intimate decked area is flanked by fruit trees and bougainvillea. Stonework troughs are filled with roses.

WEST COAST COOL Metalwork 1960s bucket chairs and a fun game of foosball against a garland of bare light bulbs and a backdrop of palm trees is the epitome of cool coastal living.

BEDROOMS

Bedrooms are not only a place to retreat to, but also the place where you spend a considerable part of your life, so decorating them in a way that makes you feel comfortable and relaxed is vital if you are going to enjoy being there.

In some ways this room has less flexibility than others when it comes to furniture layout. The bed is naturally a dominant presence in most bedrooms, so it is important to think about how much you wish to emphasize or disguise it. Storage is the other important element in planning your bedroom space. Clothes, shoes, coats etc. all need to be accommodated, even in a small space so here is where you can get creative in figuring out how and where to incorporate your clothes into the scheme. Whatever style you opt for, start by drawing up a plan of your space and working out what should go where.

SLEEPING SPACES are all about the bed and storage space. These are the key considerations whether you are designing a room from scratch or remodelling an existing space. Bed-heads, bed dressing and what type of bed to choose are all big questions to ask yourself, because the look of the bed will most likely be the biggest influence in how the room feels.

Ideal components The classic arrangements of bed, wardrobe, chest of drawers and a dressing table that form a diamond shape are the basis of best bedroom design. Where space is limited you can ration yourself to a bed plus wardrobe and drawers, employing the surface of the chest of drawers as a dressing table, or even a bed and wardrobe only in tiny spaces.

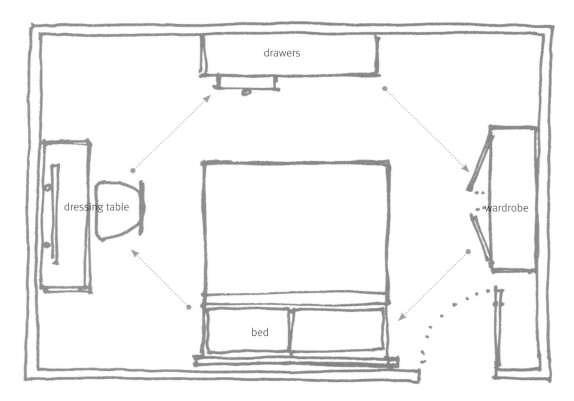

FLAMING GROOVY *Opposite* Jonathan Adler and Simon Doonan have tucked their bed into an alcove that is lined with fabric, in the French style. The same fabric is used on the lampshade and the closet panels to give a sense of uniformity.

'I love the bedroom. No matter how pared down and simply or perfectly designed a bedroom is, if you have soft pillows and pretty sheets, lights with a dimmer on them and a vase of fresh flowers, you have a sanctuary.' *Celerie Kemble, designer*

Bedroom Layouts

*Play with scale and placement to
create interesting, romantic rooms*

Work around the bed to create a
layout that enhances a beautiful
bed or disguises a nondescript
one. Use bed covers, cushions, bolsters and bedheads to set the scene and employ
colour as a tool to make a feature of the bed as a centrepiece in the room. More than
anything though, aim to end up with a calm and sensuous place, a room where the
cares of the day can disappear quickly each evening.

'The bedroom in my Sydney apartment was
inspired by a headscarf, a pair of shoes and
some nail polish that I had in my suitcase
when I arrived.' *Marie Nichols, stylist*

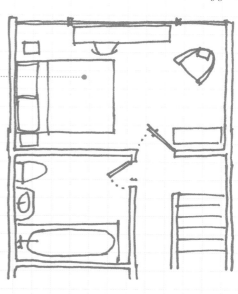

MODERN SIMPLICITY *Above* To capitalize on a great view over the whole of London the bed is placed so its inhabitants can enjoy the skyline night or day through the big picture windows. A mid-century dressing table fits neatly underneath the window so as not to block the view, while a discreet bedside table is also of low height.

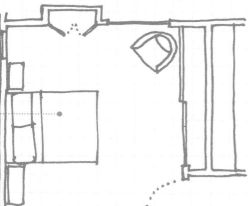

CITRUS AND RASPBERRY *Opposite* In a zingy bedroom, colour unites several different elements into a balanced whole. A lime chandelier is as much a focal point as the bed that sits squarely in the room. Citrus green is picked up in the details of framed *Vogue* magazine covers, the portrait above the bed and on the bedlinen and carpet.

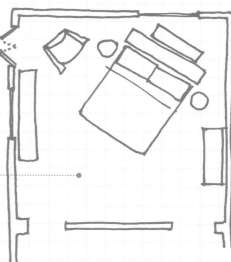

ANGLED ELEGANCE *Left* The grey upholstered bed appears to float within this loft space, with storage contained behind a partial wall at the back of the bed. In a square space, placing furniture at an angle creates some visual interest. And here the bed upholstery also softens the industrial space.

Beds & Bedding *Dress your bed in the same way you would a sofa in the living room*

The best beds always look at home in the bedroom, whether they are four posters, cabin beds, upholstered or wooden sleigh beds, their style and design blending in with the space. Look through magazines and at websites for information about all the different types of beds available. Measure your space to decide how big a bed you can fit in, then consider how to dress it.

NAUTICAL SLEEP *Above* A guest bedroom always benefits from compact storage solutions and neat, simple bedlinen. Blue and white cotton combinations are always fresh and appealing.

In small rooms, a simple divan is often the best choice as it takes up less space. Think, too, about cabin beds or else some kind of built-in underbed storage if you have no space for a decent-sized wardrobe. Plain four-poster frames with no adornment work well in all-white bedrooms, while wooden headboard and footboard arrangements are best for people who are not too tall.

DRESSING THE BED

If you go for coordinated bedlinen all in one colour, especially white, add some interest to the bed by adding on a faux fur throw.

Make a feature of the pillows, especially on a plain divan, by combining two to three pillows of varying sizes on each side of the bed. Pick out the smallest pillow in a different colour.

Layer textures to create a sense of opulence, such as a glossy satin bedspread topped with a mohair throw, or smart white Egyptian cotton finished off with a delicate linen fringed throw.

Quilts are a big feature in their own right. Handstitched patchwork quilts or striped or checked machined versions will always stand out in a bedroom.

Headboards can be specially made, customized or covered with fabric to create the right feel.

Bedlinen is one of life's necessities and one of its luxuries. Choose monogrammed or embroidered bedlinen for a special treat.

'The five most important things for a bedroom are a great reading light, wonderful linens, a dressing table, artwork and a soft rug under the bed.'

Ruthie Sommers, designer

MAJESTIC SLUMBER Liz Bauer's fleur-de-lis shaped bedhead in buttonback white silk provides a luxurious backdrop to white monogrammed bedlinen on her studio apartment bed. Opulence in a small space is all the more appealing as it is slightly unexpected.

BEDROOM STORAGE

Making sure you have enough storage for all your clothes and shoes is a top priority in the bedroom. But it does not have to mean an off-the-peg solution. Hiring a carpenter to make a storage system to your own design is also possible, particularly if you have irregular or large spaces to fill.

Dutch designer Stephanie Rammeloo commissioned storage for her stylish home created out of a converted elementary school. 'When we bought it, there were two classrooms with the adjoining wall already knocked out, part of the hallway, three small toilets and a storage room. I saw it as my opportunity to put all my ideas into action, a project that I could really get my teeth into,' says Stephanie.

COOL BLUE AND SORTED *Opposite*
Stephanie Rammeloo commissioned floor-
to-ceiling storage cupboards to her own
specification – a good idea for awkward
or non-standard spaces. The relief pattern
was added before they were painted.

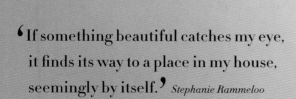

'If something beautiful catches my eye,
it finds its way to a place in my house,
seemingly by itself.' *Stephanie Rammeloo*

STORAGE NOOKS *This page* Individual nooks
were incorporated into a new dividing wall
to make neat display units for Stephanie's
ceramics collection. Glimpsed beyond are
more shelves used for shoe storage, with the
higher ones accessed by a ladder.

'I am slightly tidier than my partner Aernoud, so I decided to design huge cupboards in the bedroom and hallway to fit in all our clutter. I love to have space around me. Real space so I can move around easily, and head space, so that I can think and be creative. In this house I have achieved both, thanks to its airy atmosphere and high ceilings.'

Built-in storage does not have to be boring. 'In my work I often use relief pattern and I really enjoy it so I wanted there to be some in our house, too,' says Stephanie. 'The pattern on the white doors is made with pieces of plywood, sometimes one layer, sometimes two or none. For the blue doors ready-made trimmings were cut to octagonal shapes by the carpenter and then stuck to the door.'

WHITE RELIEF *Left* In a storage area off the bedroom, tall floor-to-ceiling cupboards and shelving house clothes and shoes as well as disguising electrical wiring and storing Stephanie's styling items.

COLOURFUL BEDROOM *Opposite* The bedroom is a warm, enclosing space painted a watery pink and furnished with a simple divan made pretty with a woollen throw. With huge storage cupboards in place there is no need for other furniture to clutter up the room.

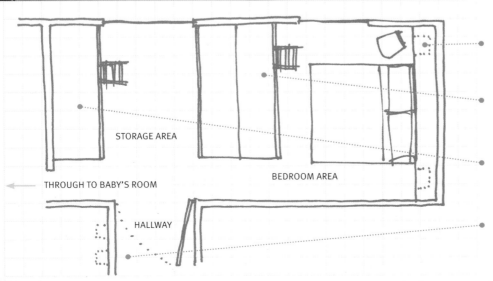

STORAGE AREA

THROUGH TO BABY'S ROOM

BEDROOM AREA

HALLWAY

A raised ledge and small nooks have been incorported behind the divan bed to provide storage and display space.

Huge floor-to-ceiling cupboards make good use of the high ceiling but do not eat up so much of the floor space.

Blue relief cupboards in the bedroom include a hand rail along the front and a sliding ladder for ease of access.

Despite all the storage cupboards the view from the hallway is a clear one, right through to the window at the end of the corridor.

'I like white in my workspace, but in the bedroom I could create a warm, lovely room. The colours remind me of the sea: the colour of the inside of a lovely shell with the cupboards being like the clear blue of the ocean. And I always think of the sea when I want to relax, so these are the best colours for a bedroom I think.' *Stephanie Rammeloo*

Bedroom Furniture

Neat ideas for furnishing your sleeping space

Pinpoint your personal bedroom style by considering what kinds of furniture you are likely to need, then search around for key pieces that will complete your desired look.

'I have probably put a custom-made storage ottoman in almost every home I have ever designed. It's great for bedrooms and for small spaces where dual functioning furniture is a must.' *Kahi Lee, designer*

SLEEP & STORAGE ESSENTIALS

Purpose-built storage is the way to go if you like to store all your clothes and shoes in one place. Allow additional space for storing out-of-season clothes.

Calculate how much clothes hanging and drawer space you need by piling up all your existing clothes, remembering to edit as you go and dispense with any you haven't worn for more than a year.

For a more eclectic approach, keep an eye out for vintage chests of drawers, shelving units and dressing tables that would make good features and also become practical storage pieces.

Customize existing built-in cupboards or freestanding furniture by painting panels or adding wallpaper or meshwork inserts, changing door knobs or adding feature handles.

Keep an eye out for footstools or ottomans for the end of the bed. You can easily reupholster them in a more contemporary fabric.

Bedside tables can range from a simple wooden table with a drawer to a contemporary Perspex cube or a circular vanity unit.

An easy chair is a great addition, not only for temporarily storing clothes, but also as a place to sit and read or dry your hair.

COSY CORNER *Above* A neat tailored grey headboard fits well with the bedlinen and lampshade in this smart, feminine bedroom. A simple bedside table has useful multiple shelves.

ROMANTIC COUNTRY *Below* White-painted vintage cupboards are a good addition to all-white country bedrooms where old paintings and an antique chair add to the charm.

REVAMPED PIECES *Above* In a contemporary space throw some quirky tradition into the mix. Here a 1930s-style chair has been reupholstered in green and repainted a bright violet colour.

TURQUOISE DISPLAY *Below* In a small bedroom a wooden display unit doubles as a linen store. Cheerful colours on furniture provide a focal point when the bed itself does not dominate.

RETRO CHIC *Above* Small dressing tables are easy to find in flea market stores and vintage emporiums. Use them to pretty up a bedroom and make an informal style statement.

MODERN TRADITION *Below* This modern take on classic 18th-century French furniture with its curved lines and sleek glossy white surface fits well in a contemporary setting.

SEAMLESS PATTERN It is hard to tell where the bed and the walls merge in this highly decorative bedroom scheme. A Jonathan Adler cushion is a witty addition to the bed itself.

EN-SUITE BEDROOM

Incorporating an en-suite bathroom into your bedroom may be as simple as a small shower room or as comprehensive as a dressing area, bath and shower combined. Whatever you have or you plan to do, think about how much space you want to devote to this important part of your bedroom when you are thinking about furniture and décor.

In Christine d'Ornano's Kensington home she decided to go bold in the bedroom, choosing Osborne & Little fabric and wallpaper to go across both the headboard and all four walls. Having been brought up in Paris, educated at Princeton in the US and spent time living in Mexico, d'Ornano has inherited a fascination for furniture and decorative objects from her parents, who have always been adventurous decorators.

'When I planned the room I knew I wanted to go with bold pattern, both on the walls and the floor. I love the end result, it makes me smile.' *Christine d'Ornano*

She loves the bright colours of Mexico, has a French flair for using fabrics on walls and is unafraid of dropping in bold designs along the way.

'My parents have always decorated with lots of colour, so that is where my bold approach comes from,' says Christine, whose father, Comte Hubert d'Ornano, co-founded Lancôme, set up Orlane and, together with his wife, Isabelle, began Sisley in 1976. 'My parents have always made joint decorating decisions, enjoying themselves in the process and I have continued the tradition with my husband, Marzouk; we are very much a team when it comes to decorating decisions.'

This is first and foremost a family home and there is evidence of the pair's three daughters' paintings and drawings in nearly every room, but especially here in the bedroom, where photos and drawings are simply pinned to the wall on either side of the bed. They are charming additions to the colourful space.

BEDSIDE STORY *Left* Amid a riot of pattern, a bedside table with a transparent top gives a sense of space next to the bed, where the walls are turned into a miniature family picture gallery.

BATHING BEAUTY *Opposite* Nestling beneath the big picture window, the bath is glimpsed from both the dressing area and the bedroom. The children's artwork forms an effortless windowsill display, completely in keeping with the décor.

An oval bath underneath the window is both a focal point and a good use of space.

Columns of clothes storage extend three-quarters of the way up the wall, library style, so as to preserve natural light and not enclose the dressing area too much.

The entrance to the en-suite dressing area and bathroom is left open so the bath and window become an enticing centrepiece glimpsed in the distance from the bed.

The bed is the main focal point in the bedroom.

BATHING AREA

SHOWER/WC

DRESSING AREA

LANDING

BEDROOM AREA

'I love the way the light pours into the bathroom and bathes the room in sunlight. This is a peaceful spot in our busy household.' *Christine d'Ornano*

BATHROOMS

Bathrooms, like kitchens, have a few key design elements that are important to think about when you are planning the space. Considerations about keeping a smooth flow between the fixtures and fittings such as sink to bath to wc need to be addressed right at the start. When there is enough space, tuck the wc out of sight as you enter the room, allowing the bath, shower or sink to take centre stage.

Lighting is important in bathrooms. Make sure the mirror over the sink has adequate (and flattering) lighting. Avoid light levels that are too harsh and introduce a relaxing mood with candles or lanterns. Adequate storage is vital in a bathroom, too. Tuck away your toiletries in a vintage cabinet or install a system of drawers or baskets. In a small space make good use of the walls rather than cluttering up the floor area.

DESIGNING A BATHROOM well is a matter of mixing function and practicality with style, and maybe some glamour thrown in too. Decide whether you are a walk-in shower person or would prefer to concentrate your design efforts on the bathtub itself. How many people will be using the room? Do you need space for a separate shower or will a bath plus shower attachment do?

A circular movement Even in the smallest bathroom there should be a natural flow between the various pieces of sanitaryware. The route between sink and bath, sink and shower and sink and WC should be easy and unimpeded, in the same way that the classic triangle layout works well in a kitchen.

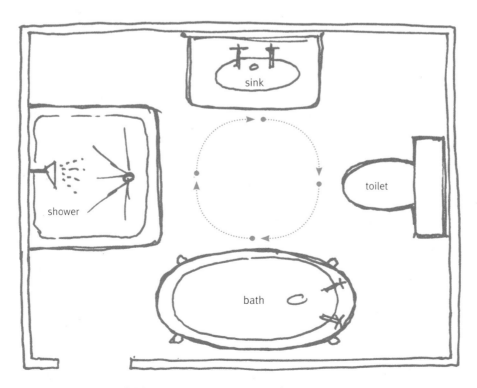

sink

shower

toilet

bath

CLEAN WHITE *Opposite* In Mairead Fanning's London home the bath is a beautiful centrepiece in a space that feels more like a chic spa than a domestic bathroom. The minimal styling is warmed through with interesting elements such as honeycomb-like tiles and a nubbly schoolhouse-style mat.

'Mix and match traditional tiles with contemporary baths or traditional baths with understated tiling to create visual interest in pale and neutral bathrooms. Choose small iridescent mosaics for half-height panelling to give an eye-catching finish in a pared-down space.'

Fired Earth

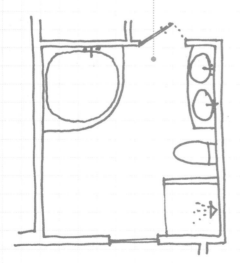

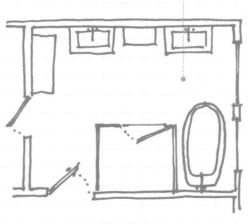

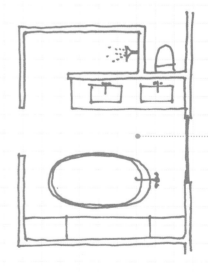

CORNER SPA *Above left* In this home a corner bath has been slipped neatly beneath the eaves to make use of an awkward space and create a cosy bathing corner. A tall, narrow plinth in sky blue mosaic tiles hides pipework and provides a ledge for displaying bathroom accessories. Corner baths are a great solution in awkward spaces.

RETRO PAIRING *Above right* A vintage vibe is created by placing a pair of retro-inspired sinks on the wall beneath large circular mirrors and separating them with a reclaimed filing cabinet. The tiles are white ceramic mosaics grouted in grey for a school washroom feel. In a large family bathroom, a separate shower and bath means family members can double up if necessary.

NEAT EN-SUITE *Opposite* A clever use of space means that two bathrooms back to back make good use of the same plumbing. A pair of sinks in this clean-lined en-suite room saves on arguments, while a feature bath is placed conveniently near by. A walk-in shower has been created behind a faux wall that adds privacy as well as becoming a room divider.

Bathroom Layouts

Creative use of every inch of space will help create the bathroom you need

In a bathroom it is important to get away from thinking you always have to use standard fixtures. Sanitaryware is available in a huge range of sizes and styles so take time to look around and find what works for you.

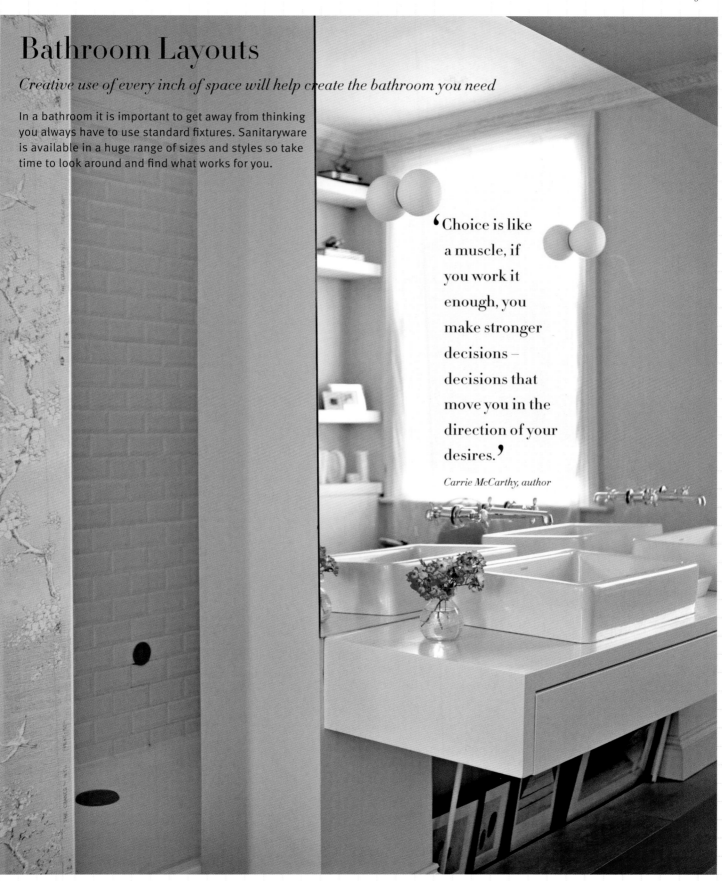

'Choice is like a muscle, if you work it enough, you make stronger decisions – decisions that move you in the direction of your desires.'

Carrie McCarthy, author

Creative Tiling *As important as paint in a living room, tiles often make a space*

Tiling is capable of utterly transforming a bathroom from a purely functional space to a colourful haven or a chic, streamlined area that conjures up a dream spa.

Tiling walls and floors in different tiles creates visual interest and is a practical design solution, particularly if you have any kind of shower. Mix and match colours, styles and size of tiles to alter the effect on the space or else go for blanket coverage for a neat, cohesive feel.

'Bathrooms and kitchens are the most important parts of a house in terms of re-sale value. They are really important rooms in the house and it is nice when they are beautiful and functional.' *Jessie Randall, designer*

FOREST GREEN *Above left* Square mosaic tiles in fern green combined with white grout has a surprisingly warming effect in a walk-in shower room. Teamed with natural wood and white walls and fixtures this is simple but effective decorating.

HERALDIC BATHING *Above right* This bathroom mixes retro styling with vintage brass fixtures and accessories that look as though they have come from Roman baths. Splashes of orange look good against the brass and prevent the room from feeling like a sea of white.

BLACK AND WHITE Tiny black slate flooring tiles teamed with white metro-style wall tiles make a clean, classic bathroom combination that is high in style as well as function. Tiling throughout in a bathroom is both useful and beautiful.

'Tiling in the bathroom is like wallpaper in a living room; it's not only a practical wall covering but can also provide a decorative edge, crisp definition or a colour statement in any bathing space.'

Fired Earth

FLOATING WALL A tall plinth forms a room divider and a wall that houses a custom-made basin and vanity unit. Behind the wall is a walk-in shower. When there is space to do so, false walls are a great idea for creating different zones of activity in bathrooms.

'The sleekness of the steel sink sitting on an old Burmese table gives you a sense of being in a foyer not a bathroom. I wanted the bathroom to have a sense of the past but read more modern.'

Vicente Wolf, designer

Basins *Choosing a basin is as much about choosing a bathroom style*

Basins are a good starting point when planning a bathroom. Gather together brochures and look at magazines and websites for ideas for different shapes and unusual materials.

If you are planning a bathroom on a tight budget, you can often save money by choosing a basic basin but splashing out on high-quality taps. But if you are set on a particularly spectacular style or shape of basin that you think will make all the difference then you can reverse the process and conserve more of your budget for that rather lovely basin or basin unit.

RETRO COASTAL *Above left* A steel industrial basin unit placed against a metal window frame and beside exposed pipework is softened by a glass cabinet displaying a collection of sea anemones and shells in Amy Neunsinger's Los Angles home.

Before you make your choice think about who will use the bathroom. A tiny ceramic bowl may look spectacular but will irritate you if several people pass through the bathroom and leave puddles of water on your countertop. Avoid low-level basins if you have a bad back, while pairs of basins are a good idea if two people get ready for work at the same time.

CHILDREN'S BATHROOM *Above right* In Anita Kauschal's London house a pair of small basins are ranged at a lower than usual height in a children's bathroom that is compact but functional. When space is tight, look for small basins that will not look too large-for the room.

Bathtubs *From freestanding to built-in, bathtubs often form the centrepiece of a bathroom*

Look out for salvaged baths to restore, designer pieces that will become covetable collectable items or choose an everyday tub and go to town on accessories.

If you are more of a shower person than an everyday bather, your bathtub may be more of a design statement than a frequently used piece of bathroom equipment, so this may colour your decision over what shape of tub to choose.

Freestanding baths are those most often used as a central feature in the room, while built-in tubs can be chosen in smaller or larger sizes than standard to fit a specific space or an awkward corner. Think about how you wish to build in a bath. You may want to incorporate a generous space for storing and displaying toiletries or else use spare space to create some pigeon-hole shelving in tiles or wood.

WHITE SPACE *Opposite* In Stephanie Rammeloo's Amsterdam loft apartment purpose-built slatted sliding doors allow natural light to flood into the compact bathroom. A standard bath appears larger due to a generous housing unit that provides extra storage at the end.

CLASSICAL BATHING *Above* Anita Kaushal's bathroom is more of a relaxing space that happens to incorporate a traditional bath rather than a functional bathroom with useful storage and display. Roll-top baths are widely available as reproductions or originals, ready for revamping.

'Bathrooms are a great place to combine natural textures and materials in refreshing ways. There are so many different approaches to the bath and I always want mine to feel like a spa.'

Amy Butler, designer

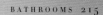

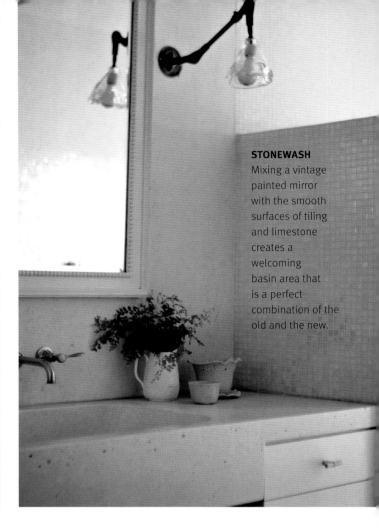

STONEWASH
Mixing a vintage painted mirror with the smooth surfaces of tiling and limestone creates a welcoming basin area that is a perfect combination of the old and the new.

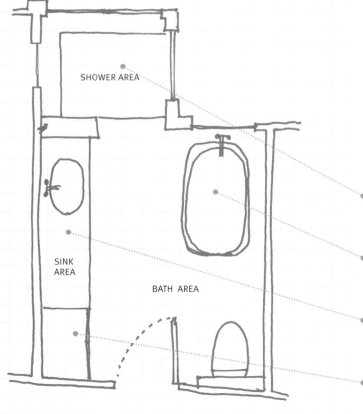

Amy Neunsinger's glamorous bathroom combines sleek lines with luxurious materials and a statement period piece. Dominating the space is a claw-footed Victorian bath that has been reconditioned, then painted a pale mushroom colour to tone well with the limestone sink unit. On the walls of the sink area and in the shower wet room are two types of mother-of-pearl mosaic tiles that reflect natural light and provide a subtle shimmer in each of the two spaces. Effortless glamour that is not too hard to achieve.

SHOWER AREA

SINK AREA

BATH AREA

Frosted windows allow natural light to flood into the fully tiled shower room. A low-level tiled area is used for storage and as a seat.

A reclaimed bath is a big feature in the room as you enter the bathroom.

A purpose-built limestone slab sink incorporates single drawers and extends along one wall.

Fabric storage boxes beneath the generous vanity surface offer access to toiletries.

ROOM WITH A VIEW
Above left A low-level reclaimed bathtub sits beneath a picture window. The painted concrete floor enhances light.

SHOWER SPACE
Opposite Frosted glass encloses the walk-in shower with its stylish showerhead and reflective walls.

CASE STUDY

LUXURY BATHROOM

Creating glamour in the bathroom is all about combining luxurious materials in an understated way to produce shimmering surfaces, inspiring textures and a dash of surprise. It need not be expensive to reproduce an air of luxury. Keep the emphasis on one or two key areas such as the bath, the sink, one-off lighting or the walls and floors to make instant glamour.

'My bathroom is filled with light, has a view of the canyons and the shower is large enough that a shower curtain is not needed.

It is luxurious and sparkly and makes me happy each time I walk in.'

Amy Neunsinger, photographer

CHILDREN'S ROOMS

Creating a children's room is one of the most fun-filled and emotionally satisfying decorating jobs you can undertake. Designing a room for your own child is your chance to express your love full-on, by putting a piece of yourself in the space.

It may be that you handcraft a quilt for the bed, or create a collage of family photos or mementos in a painted frame, or take footprints or handprints of your child as a baby and display these alongside a first pair of shoes or valued trophies. Whatever touches your inner decorator, use it to connect with your children in their own rooms. This is one space where you can let all your colour whims go wild because kids love colour. Incorporate a comfortable and cosy sleeping space, somewhere to store and display toys that the kids can have access to and, for older children, a desk.

DESIGNING CHILDREN'S ROOMS allows you the chance to think about your own childhood and pass on anything you remember with fondness to the next generation. You may have had a favourite chest of drawers in a particular colour or a set of display shelves with mementos from holidays. Allow the space to grow with your child and enjoy watching the process.

Growing needs If you don't want to be altering your child's room each year as they grow too quickly, take some time to plan for the transition from the cot to the toddler bed to the teenager daybed. Constant change and flexibility are required when it comes to designing children's rooms, so bear this is mind before you jump headfirst into a particular age-related look or style.

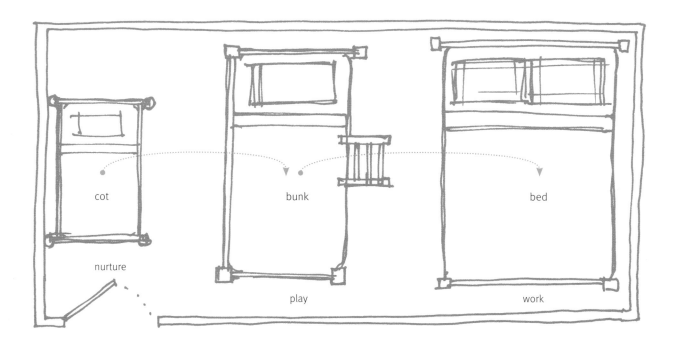

cot

nurture

bunk

play

bed

work

PLAYSPACE *Opposite* Just as important as children's bedrooms are playspaces elsewhere in the home. They can be as simple as a corner of a kitchen or eating area or as complex as a specially decorated playroom.

'I think it is very
important that
children have a place to
create, to play, to learn.
Ideally with a window,
because of the natural
light and nature.'

Jenny Levié, editor in chief

CASE STUDY

GIRL'S ROOM

Girls' bedrooms need to reflect the passions and pastimes of the inhabitants. Try not to get too hung up on creating a specific theme. Children's tastes change and develop at a much faster rate than adults, so it's best to avoid spending a lot of time slavishly creating a certain look only for it to become outdated or unloved within months. Girls like to be involved in decorating decisions so talk to your daughter about what she sees or likes. Encourage her to create her own scrapbook of favourite images to help her formulate her own visual sense.

Leslie Shewring, a freelance photographer and stylist, chose not to introduce a specific theme into her daughter's room but instead let her daughter collect together the things she liked, including some art from her mother's own collection. 'Occasionally I buy little prints that fit in with themes she is interested in, such as carousels or cupcakes, as well as things that are not toys; things such as nesting dolls or containers, sparkly figures or little decorated boxes that she can hide things in. I made a simple covered headboard to line the wall so there are no hard surfaces for when she is running and jumping on the beds. Of course, it is always nice to have an extra bed in a child's room for when family or friends are visiting.'

'I decided to place two low platform beds end to end because it creates a long soft space to hang out on and read or play. It is similar to a long wide sofa and who doesn't like lounging on something like this with lots of cushions?'

Leslie Shewring

DAY BED It's important to provide a comfortable lounging space so that children always feel at home in their rooms. As they get older and become teenagers their rooms become important sanctuaries, so keep them smart and inviting for as long as possible.

TIMELESS APPEAL *Above and opposite*
Decorating a child's room without age-specific elements allows you to experiment more with art and accessories. As long as you incorporate a comfortable bed, adequate storage and plenty of playspace, the room will always work for your child.

Girls particularly enjoy having friends to sleep over so, if you can, incorporate space for additional sleeping equipment. Make full use of the height of the room. Consider installing a bunk bed or a cabin bed with space beneath for an extra mattress. A truckle bed with a mattress tucked onto a wheeled platform for pulling out when guests appear is a space-saver.

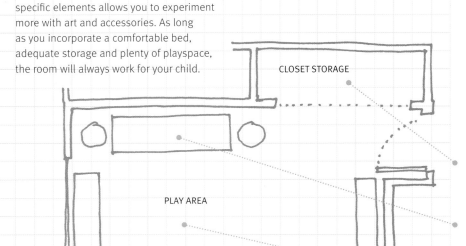

CLOSET STORAGE

PLAY AREA

BED

SLEEPOVER BED

Storage is key in a child's room: toys, clothes, a dressing-up box and games all need to be kept in an accessible place.

A chest of drawers is versatile for storing smaller items and for display.

Allow some space as a flexible play area for board games, a small desk and chair, jigsaws or play figures.

If space allows, incorporate a spare bed for sleepovers and guests.

'I like the idea of displaying things that are curious for her but are not toys.' *Leslie Shewring*

Rooms for All Ages

Create a room that can grow with your child

Ring the age changes by repainting a wall or some furniture in a newly favoured colour, changing what is hanging on the wall or introducing a new, more grown-up bed.

'I like the way that using old toys in children's rooms gives them a sense of the past when they are bombarded with mass-produced TV characters today. Old toys are often very charming and don't necessarily need to be collector's items.' *Emily Dyson, designer*

FLEXIBLE DECORATING IDEAS

For toddlers choose a bed that can grow with them. An antique sleigh bed or one layer of a bunk bed may make them look tiny when asleep at first, but the bed will see them through a good five or six years' worth of life.

Paint one wall of the room in a strong colour that your child loves. Keep checking back with them that they still love it and if not, repaint it or wallpaper over it.

Learning and decorating can go hand in hand. Paper one wall with a huge map of the world, scientific symbols or hang retro posters depicting flora and fauna.

Notice what your children respond to in art galleries or museums and take something home with you for their rooms. Just because they're children doesn't mean they can't appreciate van Gogh or the Impressionists, for instance.

Personalize a room by incorporating your child's name on wall-hung letters, as monograms on cushions, pillows or towels, or painted onto a piece of furniture.

Create an heirloom for your child – a patchwork quilt, a handmade toy box or dolls' house, a wooden miniature chair, a framed print of family mementos or a favourite childhood toy displayed in a box frame.

Make sure you include a place to display your children's art. It encourages creativity and boosts their confidence to know their efforts are valued.

COLOURFUL CHEST *Above*
Painted furniture is a quick and easy way of ringing the changes in a child's room. Paint it in your child's favourite colours or in shades that suit the room.

PINK HAVEN *Below* Rather than turning a room into a pink palace, paint one wall only and use pretty accessories such as blankets and floral cushions to continue the feminine theme.

BUNKING DOWN *Above* Space-saving and a perennial children's favourite, bunk beds are cosy, fun and inviting, whatever time of the day. Add integral shelving and lighting where possible.

THROUGH THE AGES *Below* This toddler's bedroom will readily adapt to a teenager's den. There is spare space that can be used for spreading out schoolwork where there are now toys.

STARS AND STRIPES *Above* A loose theme can be achieved with accessories in particular colours. Changes can be easily made when your child outgrows or becomes bored with the look.

PERSONAL SPACE *Below* Make a feature of the bed by painting an antique sleigh bed and placing it in a dominant space in the room beneath your child's name. No mistaking who lives in this space.

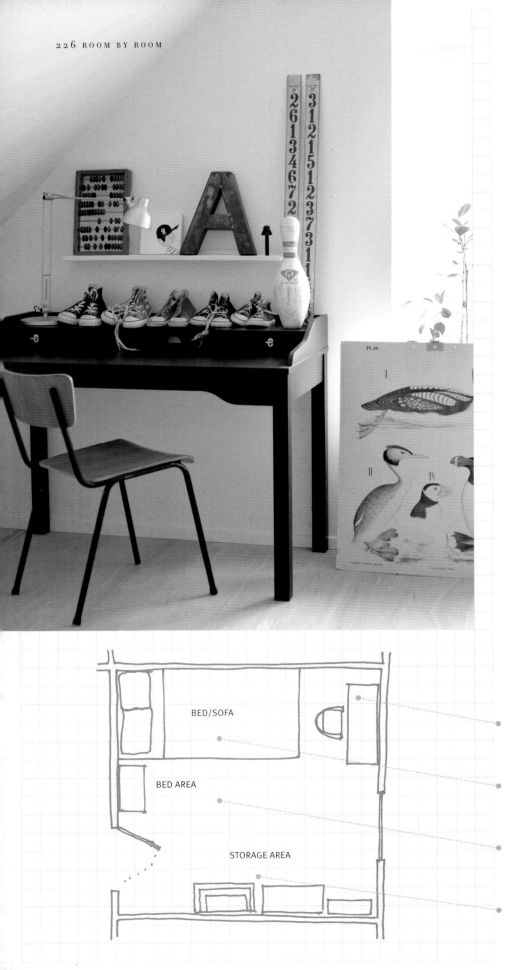

Former Montessori school teacher turned illustrator Anna-Malin Lindgren created an interesting bedroom first and a masculine boy's space second, so that the room can be adapted very easily in the future as her son grows into a teenager. A metal-framed bed is decorated with a collection of customized cushions and a nautical duvet, whose theme is reinforced by some pirate bunting and a string of rope suspended from the eaves, ship style, to display her son's artwork and quirky bits and pieces. A collection of vintage suitcases piled on the floor continues both the seafaring theme and the vintage feel of the room.

WORKING OUT *Left* A collection of sneakers decorates the top of a useful bureau that can be used for homework and creative activities. Wooden floors make sense in children's rooms where spills are inevitable.

AHOY THERE *Opposite* A sophisticated take on the traditional nautical boy's room theme, the decorating is all done with accessories, which will make it easily adaptable later on.

BED/SOFA

BED AREA

STORAGE AREA

A desk space is really useful in a child's room, even if it comprises just a tiny desk and a folding chair.

A metal-framed bed is robust and allows for some underbed storage space.

Keep some space free in the centre of the room for toy soldiers, board games and playspace for when friends visit.

Devote a wall to storage, either freestanding or built-in.

BOY'S ROOM

Boys often like their bedrooms to include space to spread out larger games and activities such as sports punch bags, Subbutteo or miniature table football and elaborate car racing tracks and vast tracts of construction bricks. Boys also tend to make use of desks, for model making for example, more than girls so bear this in mind when setting out to plan and decorate their space.

CREATIVE SPACES

If you work from home and are creative it is so important to have a space you can call your own. Somewhere that is calm and light-filled ideally, with plenty of storage space and as generous a desk as you can manage. A place to display ideas and inspiration is also key, and don't forget to incorporate some favourite things to cheer you when your inspiration wanes or to encourage the ideas to flow.

Make a list of what equipment you need for your creative work, whether it is floristry or art, writing or typography, ceramics or sewing, then work out where the best place in your home is to create a space that will enable you to feel both inspired and at home and comfortable.

WORKING AREAS can be designed in the smallest of spaces if needs be: in walk-in closets, behind false walls in a bedroom or living room, on a fold-down table in a kitchen cupboard or in self-contained purpose-built spaces in the garden or an outhouse. Wherever there are a few square metres of space, you can set up a workstation, whether it is temporary or permanent, tiny or palatial.

Practical planning Sort out which items of furniture will take precedence – a large desk for spreading out plans and paperwork or a huge cupboard to fit in oversized tools or containers? Do you need a whole wall of display space for your ideas? Do you need a desk and a dedicated worktop for things like sewing or for spreading out reference material and brochures?

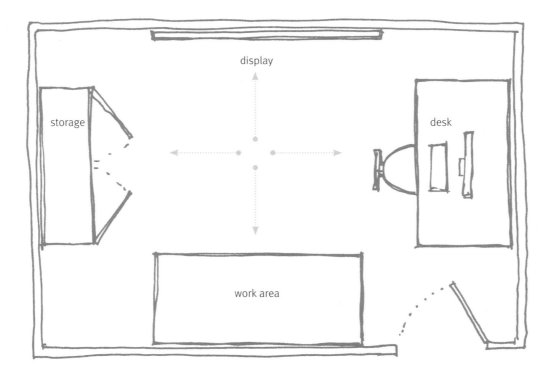

SEW CREATIVE *Opposite* Virginia Armstrong's sewing desk is a simple trestle table that can be taken down when the space is needed for something else. Wall shelves provide a permanent place for ever-changing displays of inspiration and a plan chest allows for the neat storage of fabric swatches and completed artworks.

'My favourite room changes all the time. It's usually the one I've just finished updating or redecorated! But that's the power of decorating – you get to put your inspirations, ideas and creativity to work to create a space that not only suits the function of the room, but your desires as well.' *Belinda Graham, blogger*

Workstations *The hub of the homeworker*

Your desk should be in a quiet place where you can concentrate, and ideally it should be away from living and sleeping areas. If you work in the kitchen you may be distracted by chores and snacks; working in a bedroom means that you can never really switch off at night, while in living rooms you could well be disturbed by other members of the family at various times of the day.

Choose a desk that suits your working needs. Writers may want the reassurance of a solid, traditional writing desk with built-in drawers for storing stationery and reference books. An artist may be better off with a tilting easel-type desk, while a florist, sewer or craftsperson could work happily at a trestle table and use the additional space below the desk for storing crates of materials. Personalize your desk with family photos or a nearby pinboard for inspiration.

MAKING SPACE FOR WORK

Choose a desk that is large enough for all your paperwork, incorporates some storage and has ample space for a computer and a printer if needed.

Lighting is important so pick a desk lamp that lights both your work surface and your computer screen effectively.

If you are working in a dual-purpose space, make sure your work desk or workstation blends in with the rest of the décor rather than standing out as a specific workspace.

Store superfluous equipment and materials behind closed doors or drawers so that you aren't distracted by clutter when you are trying to concentrate.

Arrange your electrical wiring and sockets so that you have easy access to the telephone, computer, lighting and music.

CREATIVE DISPLAY *Above* Keep photos and significant pieces of inspiration close by as you work. They provide a visual breather as well as inspiration when you are immersing yourself in a work project.

'A nice workspace at home will encourage you to use your talents and give more structure to your ideas and work schedule. Working in a nice atmosphere will always bring out the best in you!'

Irene Hoofs, blogger

SCHOOLHOUSE WORKHOUSE In Stephanie Rammeloo's converted schoolhouse in Amsterdam, her workspace forms one wall of the large living space so is designed to fit in rather than stand out from the space. Ample storage in the form of freestanding pieces slipped underneath a long run of worktop means that the work surface itself is kept for paperwork.

'Living and working under the same roof has many advantages for family life, providing short routes from the office to the workshop to the kitchen.'

Claudia Nowotny, store owner

DISPLAY AND STORAGE *Opposite top left* In Leslie Shewring's Californian home she has devoted a whole room to her creative space. Here she stores all her fabric samples, ribbons and other sewing materials together with vases and containers relating to her passion for flower arranging.

COSY STUDY *Opposite top right* Christine d'Ornano's husband, Marzouk, has added a compact study next door to the bedroom, dressing area and en-suite bathroom. The walls are lined with deep turquoise linen for a clubby, cosy feel. Here he can catch up on paperwork or watch TV in a dedicated space adjacent to the bedroom.

PINK DISPLAY *Opposite bottom left* Sabine Brandt's work desk nestles under the eaves in a converted bedroom where one sugar pink wall provides a gallery-like backdrop to a personal display of photographs, art and collections.

WHITE LIBRARY *Opposite bottom right* In this tall room, the office of Amy Neunsinger's husband, Shawn Gold, floor-to-ceiling shelves are a good way of storing and displaying a vast collection of vintage and leather-bound books. Access is via a library ladder.

VINTAGE INVENTIVE *This page* Any corner of a room can be turned into an appealing workspace with a movable trestle table, an interesting chair and an array of creative accessories.

Lyndsay is a metalsmith and Fitzhugh a sculptor and designer, so they have made every bit of space work for them to allow plenty of white shelving for displaying their design experiments and inspiration. 'White can lend itself to anything, for us it's the perfect backdrop to the things we make and collect.'

The rest of the space is an informal living area so the idea of working along one long wall of the room aids their concentration as there is no view to distract them from work. Small filing cabinets are slotted beneath the worktop for storing files and paperwork and a smart iroko worktop makes a wonderful long run of desktop space.

HOME WORK *Left* Make yourself at home at your desk by displaying photos, treasured objects and reference materials. Make space for reminder notes as well as exercise books for writing down ideas when they come into your head.

A WALL OF WORK *Opposite* A space-saving home office was created with a bespoke pigeon-hole shelving system and a wooden worktop, with built-in cupboards and freestanding storage slotted in between two side-by-side work desks.

WORK AREA SHELVING

HALLWAY TO GARDEN

GUEST SUITE STORAGE

GARDEN ROOM

A space-saving workstation is ranged along one wall, with chairs tucked under the work surface when not in use.

If you position a desk away from a window you won't be distracted when working, but allow adequate artificial light.

A dedicated storage space is tucked away from the work area and houses larger materials for sculpture, metalwork and design.

The guest suite tucks away discreetly behind the work area.

WORKING FROM HOME

When you do not have to step out of your front door to get to your office it's important to have a dedicated space in your home that you can still refer to as your workplace. Create somewhere in which you can store, retrieve and process all the necessary equipment and materials for your job, a place where you keep the personal tools of your trade. Psychologically and physically it is always good to have a distinct area that is for work alone, but it is also perfectly possible to create a work corner by adding a screen to divide off the space or to have a movable, easily portable desk.

Lyndsay Caleo and Fitzhugh Karol have dedicated the garden level floor of their Brooklyn home to an informal workspace and a guest suite. This arrangement is perfect for working from home as it is calm and quiet, with immediate access to the garden and plenty of natural light, while at night and over weekends it switches function to become a perfect guest suite.

'We have deliberately used white as the backdrop to this space because with all the information we take in visually every day, white on white is a resting place. The right white is timeless.'

Lyndsay Caleo and Fitzhugh Karol

"It's the **finishing touches** that add the wow factor and take any room from ORDINAIRE to extra-ordinaire."

Abigail Ahern

Attention to Detail

'Jonathan uses our pad as a canvas for his design ideas.'

Simon Doonan, creative director/author

ARTFUL DISPLAY *Previous page* On a mantelpiece or shelf create
a still life from collected and found objects. Flora and fauna,
haberdasher's silks, discarded price signs and battered picture
frames make a cohesive display united by colour and texture.

'Our stuff is constantly changing and evolving as
I make new things and new collections. My poor,
long-suffering husband never knows when a beloved
ceramic piece, sofa or lamp is gonna' disappear and
be switched with something new.'

Jonathan Adler, potter/interor designer

CERAMIC SHELVING *This page* Group a collection of
ceramics according to height, function, style or colour.
Play around with the positioning until you are happy you
have the perfect arrangement.

CREATING FINISHING TOUCHES

Once you have planned your space and furnished it with the things you love and long to surround yourself with, you can start to think about the all-important finishing touches. It is the details in a space that can provide an elusive harmony, a perfect colour commentary or a quirky decorative touch that may lift a room from the mundane to the magical.

Look around you and sort through your belongings to pinpoint the items that make an emotional connection with you. It may be a family holiday photo in a battered frame, a child's drawing or artwork, a gifted plant from a friend or a treasured object brought back from your travels that is shouting out to have some shelf space.

APPRECIATING HOW MUCH IMPACT can be achieved by carefully choosing and creating finishing touches is an important part of decorating. Whether it is a decorative light fitting, a textured throw or rug, a small collection of painted picture frames or small detailing such as piping on an upholstered chair or a delicate ceramic bowl on display, the details all count.

Icing on the cake When you look around a newly decorated room, is it calling out for a bit of love and attention? Does it seem a little too pared down or a little too perfect? Does it need warming up with a rug or two? Do you have enough sofa cushions and throws? Is your lighting a little lacking? Think about how you can make the details start working harder for you.

LIGHTING DETAIL *This page* Introduce some decorative detail in the form of wall lights to create some drama in a bedroom. This glamorous piece definitely adds pizzazz to floral wallpaper and a plain pearl balloon blind.

BEDROOM FINISH *Opposite* Layering fabrics is a good way to finish a bed and make a decorative statement in a bedroom. Pile up a variety of cushions as well as placing a bedspread on top of a quilt on top of a bedcover to create a visual story.

'The last few layers of any space are the most aesthetically important as these are the details that truly personalize the room and bring out its soul. For texture, warmth and a pop of colour, add decorative cushions and handmade rugs. In the end, it's about creating rooms that reflect you, your life and your personality.'

Thom Filicia, designer

The Art of Arrangement

Creating impact with display

'Grouping art collections on a wall works so well, because just by sheer numbers you can make a strong visual statement. Some might recommend three to five pieces on a wall ... I say more is more!'

Christina Batch-Lee, Etsy

Grouping together collections of objects is a stylist's dream but can sometimes be a source of confusion for a home decorator. Should you place picture frames all the same together or vary the shapes, colours and sizes? Would a mix of old and new chairs work better than a purely vintage line-up? Is it better to cram a shelf, tabletop or mantelpiece full of objects in the hope that one of them stands out from the crowd or should you aim for a discreet display of three objects?

As a general rule, grouping similar objects together in groups of three works better than a pair of things. Eclectic collections supply visual interest and random picture frames look perfectly fine as long as there is variety to create an engaging visual feast. When displaying only a few objects, make sure they are in keeping with the overall style of a room. Three church candles on a mantelpiece will look good in a simply styled room, for instance, but will get lost in a room where riotous colours dominate.

GROUP PICTURE *Left* A lined-up display works best if all the individual elements are quite different from one another. In Vicente Wolf's New York loft he has ranged a collection of black and white photographs along two seamless shelves to create a gallery beneath which many styles of occasional chair make a witty parade.

ART GALLERY *Opposite* Rita Konig prefers a random grouping of images above a fireplace. A mix of canvasses and framed paintings carry a subject matter of flowers and nature. Grouping items by theme can work well.

'There is nothing quite like original art on the walls and it doesn't have to cost a bomb. Go to second-hand shops and garage sales for bargain finds. Don't shop at one store – you will end up looking like a catalogue. Don't forget the meaningful elements that make a space a home.' *Deborah Bibby, editor in chief*

Make sure that there is some consistency in your arrangement. It may be colour, shape or material that is the unifying element. Or it could be a collection of similar items such as chairs, cushions or candles. Consider the height and scale of objects, too, as this is another way of creating impact.

Once you have arranged your objects to your liking you could consider lighting them from above or below if they are on a shelf or provide some background light if they are placed on the floor. An angled spotlight from the ceiling would work well for a wall display, especially of paintings and artwork.

GLASS ARRAY *Above* Jonathan Adler's collection of 1960s Venetian glassware is humorous and colourful against white walls and fireplace in a traditional room. They are as unexpected as they are funny.

Colour groupings work well for glass, especially on mantels and window ledges. Arrange statement pieces in a simple line and close to natural light for maximum impact.

Good display is often about injecting some humour into your collections. Glass and ceramics with faces, a collection of wind-up toys in a grown-up space or some quirky vintage black-and-white magazine advertisements in frames are all examples of a lighter touch.

Natural objects are obvious candidates for striking collections. Sea shells, greenery, tracery leaves and forest finds such as pine cones are unselfconscious display items.

For pictures, place them in frames that are also decorative. Arrange smaller frames on a side table or windowsill but allow larger ones more space. Spread them out across one wall or lean oversized pieces against a spare wall for a gallery feel.

Unexpected artefacts are great for drawing attention to themselves. Retro kitchenalia, 1960s glassware, faux vintage flowers, bright textiles and stylized emblematic cushions are all unusual but effective objects for display.

Use houseplants for a green approach to display. Group together a couple of large-scale plants with bold leaves such as fig or rubber plants and stand them behind some feather ferns or hardy spider plants. Retro but eco.

AUTUMNAL GLASS *Opposite* Modern-day interpretations of apothecary jars have a delightful decorative pharmacy feel to them. Vivid colours and a lot of detailing make them ideal for a striking window display.

'Soulful interiors are built over time by finding pieces that speak to your taste, style and experiences.'

Michelle Adams, designer

'There is strength in numbers. Two tchotchkes on a shelf is nothing to mention; twenty matching tchotchkes on a shelf is a collection! A cohesive theme is key to letting a collection stand out.' *Christina Batch-Lee, Etsy*

ETHNIC DIVERSITY The fruits of a well-travelled existence form a smart display on these white shelves. Astier de Villatte ceramics from the South of France mingle with a Buddha from the Far East, Danish ceramics, Indonesian batik templates and inherited pewter. The colour white acts as a unifying element.

CONCRETE SHELF LIFE *Above*
Heavy concrete shelving is suspended on metal brackets and houses a collection of eclectic ceramics, with a trailing plant providing some greenery.

VINTAGE COLLECTION *Below* A varied selection of decanters, vases and ice buckets from the 1950s and 1960s have a superb 'look at us' moment on plain white open display shelving.

EMOTIONAL REUNION *Above*
Sania Pell has taken the time to box frame her child's first cardigan and shoes and placed them in a bedroom on a wall of very personal mementos.

DROP ME A LINE *Below*
Displaying greetings cards and postcards in a kitchen is a good way of keeping your friends and family close by if you live far away from them.

DECORATIVE DISTRESS *Above left* A console table with elegant tapered legs, painted a smart shade of grey and distressed makes a traditional statement in a modern home.

SMALL OBJECTS *Below* Religious and other figurines mingle with a collection of miniature designer vases in a mantel display that hints of humour in Rita Konig's New York apartment.

PSYCHEDELIC GLASS *Above right* Streamlined glass vases in browns, greens and white make a bold display on top of an ironwork mantel. Colour, form and scale all come into play here.

CABIN CLASS *Opposite* Thom Filicia creates comfortable classicism in a lake house, where the spoils of hunting are proudly displayed on a wooden wall in a statement of rural living.

'My aesthetic is to combine classic simplicity with a modern flair.'

Thom Filicia, designer

MIRRORS

Reflect on

Mirrors are a great way of allowing more light into a space, especially hallways and dark spaces where natural light needs encouragement, and are decorative items in their own right. Scout around for interesting vintage pieces or go shoppingc for modern mirrors. There is a vast variety of shapes, sizes, frames and surrounds to choose from. If you know the style you are searching for, visit salvage yards or flea markets to find them. Or ask a designer to create a bespoke mirror if you cannot find what you're looking for.

'Even if your relatives have boring taste, or no taste at all, I promise there is a treasure lurking in the attic somewhere – even if it's just an old suitcase that suddenly looks super-chic – there is at least one nugget of beauty in every home.' *Tori Mellott, style writer*

'Mirrors and lighting give depth to all spaces.'

Lulu deKwiatkowski, designer

GLAMOUR SUNBURST *This page top* Jonathan Adler's vintage sun mirror has a porthole-style glass that makes a fish bowl of the games room glimpsed through it.

CHROME WREATH MIRROR *This page bottom* This striking Rain Drops mirror was made from antiqued chrome and mirror glass, signed and dated by the metalwork artist of wall sculptures and household accessories C. Jeré.

RETRO REFLECTION *Opposite top* Group a collection of vintage mirrors on a bedroom wall to create impact and interest, the greater variety of shapes the better.

FRENCH FANCY *Opposite bottom left* A matching mirror and display make an ornate statement next to a faux traditional fireplace. Such frilly furniture usually works best in spaces without too much extraneous detailing to provide distraction.

GOTHIC SPLENDOR *Opposite bottom right* An ecclesiastical take on a dress mirror provides enough decoration in a relatively underdressed room; however, a ceramic poodle is sneaking a peek in case things change without notice.

LIGHTING

Decorative lighting is often much more than a finishing touch. Making a big deal of a pendant light can become a significant point of interest in a room. Look at the huge range of contemporary new fittings as well as vintage finds for your inspiration.

FIFTIES GLAMOUR *Right* Vintage finds add a touch of glamour when reconditioned and fitted with up-to-date bulbs. Adjust flexes so they fit in with existing ceiling features such as ceiling roses.

BULB CHIC *Below left* New meets old in a witty take on the bare light bulb look. This lighting has the advantage of being both temporary and movable, so it's a good idea as a stopgap while waiting for your dream flea market find to come along.

THE PERFECT FINALE *Below right* A French-style chandelier conjures up thoughts of patisseries and lively parlours. It works well against a backdrop of intricate architectural detailing in a period living space.

'Because lighting makes such a statement in a room, it should be incorporated into a design scheme from the beginning.'

Marcia Zia-Priven, lighting designer

DANISH MODERN This classic light design from Poul Henningsen, the PH Artichoke light, was designed decades ago for a Copenhagen restaurant, where the originals still hang. It looks equally good in hallways, above dining tables and in living spaces.

GLASS DANCE *Right* Ochre's Light Drizzle chandelier is a covetable contemporary piece made from polished nickel and clear glass drops. It is glamorous enough to grace a simple living space as much as a more ornate dining area.

FRENCH VINTAGE *Below right* Table lamps with ornate bases are making a comeback for providing a decorative flourish in living and dining spaces. This metal base of spring anemones is pretty and colourful.

'Lighting should be considered the jewellery of the home. It evokes emotion.'

Marcia Zia-Priven, lighting designer

'You can find so many amazing lamps online – just search and you will be amazed at what you find.' *Vanessa De Vargas, designer*

LIGHT UP YOUR LIFE

Decorative chandeliers make all the difference to a living space or kitchen/diner. Make sure you also have adequate task or accent lighting elsewhere in the room: either recessed spots, worktop lighting or floor lamps.

A room with an overhead pendant or chandelier plus several table lamps and maybe a floor lamp will always feel more welcoming than a room with harsh overhead lighting and no pools of interest.

Add drama by including uplighters, downlighters or recessed lights to highlight architectural features such as fireplaces and arches or to pinpoint specific pieces such as pictures or sculptures.

Lighting can be dramatic if you choose a huge chandelier, either bespoke or ready-made.

Make table lamps a decorative feature as well as a light source by placing them prominently on console tables, side tables or desks.

Retro desk lamps and table lamps look equally at home in a modern apartment or in a country cottage, as their clean, classic lines work in both types of home.

If you are displaying items on recessed shelves or in glass-fronted cupboards, create some drama by adding lighting at the front or the back of the objects, or else as down lighting or edging lighting.

'Lighting can change the entire mood of a room and be very inexpensive to change with dimmers, bulb covers or new shades.' *Rachel Ashwell, designer*

SMOKED GLASS FLORAL Glass bases are classy affairs, especially teamed with contrasting lampshades in country florals or complementary colours to the base. They provide as much decoration as they do a light source, especially in bedrooms and living rooms.

CUSHIONS

Providing comfort, colour and individual design touches, cushions are a perfect way of shifting the colour balance of a room, ringing seasonal changes, dressing up worn or ugly seating, altering the look of a bedroom for a minimal outlay – and making you smile on a daily basis.

MID-CENTURY GRAPHICS *Right* Roddy & Ginger textiles mingle with other graphic patterns on a classic Ercol sofa in Virginia Armstrong's London home. Picking out two base colours, then decorating with cushions that combine the two of them is tonally pleasing without being too matchy-matchy.

TEXTURAL LAYERS *Below left* Mix and match colours and patterns, then add in some texture to create an additional layer of comfort on clean-lined furniture in a neutral space.

WHITE ON WHITE *Below right* Mix up cushion shapes, especially when they are of a similar colour. Here a knitted ribbed square cushion adds a certain softness when placed behind a circular ruffled silk grey cushion.

'Cushions can add a bit of flavour to a neutral scheme and give it personality. Hand embroidered and vintage pieces become cherished heirlooms, inspiring colour palettes and room themes, and adding originality to your home' *Niki Jones, designer*

'Always keep an eye on the detail. Finishing touches such as throws and cushions make all the difference, especially in the bedroom.' *Nate Berkus, designer*

EDGY DESIGN Piping on bed cushions provides graphic definition and here gives a unifying finish to a collection including a jazzy needlepoint design and a selection from Ferm Living in different styles, from floral fabric and plain velvet to graphic motifs.

FLOWERS

Flowers are the costume jewellery of the home. A small detail, perhaps, yet one that can totally transform a room in the way a glittery necklace lifts the game of a black dress. Chosen with care, flowers are a powerful decorating tool and floral design a wonderful form of self-expression.

SPRING POPPIES *Right* Place brightly coloured flowers in plain white vases for a maximum colour statement. These multi-toned papery poppies will brighten up anyone's day when placed on a dinner table or hallway table.

ROSES AND PEONIES *Below left* If you love the effect of metal vases, slip a smaller vase inside, otherwise the metal will shorten their shelf life. Here a tight arrangement of mustard-coloured dahlias complement the deep and soft pinks of roses and peonies.

HAZY DAISY *Bottom right* Simple gerberas look like something special having been placed in a Jonathan Adler container next to a golden-coloured reflective ribbed vase. A case of less is more with the right vase.

'Remember a few fresh flowers! I have always picked little sprigs to put into tiny vases and I find them hard to resist at the grocery store because flowers feel like home and they brighten any corner.'

Leslie Shewring, photographer/stylist

COUNTRY RAINBOW
Create an informal vibe by loosely placing cottage-garden flowers in a vintage enamelware vase for a delightful summer lunch party or simply to liven up the kitchen table.

Displaying Flowers

Experiment with your flowers. Gather a collection of favourite vases, make a list of flowers you are drawn to and the colours that work in each room of your house, then enjoy the process of mixing and matching blooms according to the season.

'Using one type of flower either en masse or in individual pots is always more arresting than a collection of colours and varieties. The repetition of an idea is a very simple yet effective way of designing with flowers.' *Paula Pryke, florist*

DIVINE ROSES This combination of sugar-plum pink roses displayed as single stems in tall glass cylinders wrapped in paper doilies, handmade sky blue papers and thin string creates a delicate still life that has a painterly quality.

THIRTIES GLAMOUR *Right* Tight rosebuds in soft pink stand out beautifully against an Art Deco inspired frosted and glazed vase. Create a complete colour story by choosing vases that contrast or tone with your flowers.

COTTAGE GARDEN *Bottom left* Green, white and yellow are among the most common colours in the garden so display flowers of these colours in soft green jugs and vases in a spring-like tableau to freshen up any space.

ROSE BOWL *Bottom right* Snip off the heads of large flowers such as roses, hydrangeas or peonies and pop them into a shallow bowl for an instant floral pick-me-up.

'Flowers can add a wonderful warmth and charm to any home. I love to celebrate the seasons with colour palettes that are appropriate to the time of year. My floral design is rooted in nature. I take cues from colour stories that occur in nature and like to arrange flowers in a flowing and natural manner.' *Pam Zsori, florist*

Containers

CANDY-COLOURED RAINBOW These allsorts glass vases in a rainbow of colours look like a candy store display all of its own, so only a few stems are needed in each vase to complete a bright and bold tableau.

Presenting flowers in pleasing containers is as important as choosing inspiring flowers in the first place. Always keep an eye out for colourful, unusual, vintage or plain vases, jugs or bowls that will set off all manner of different blooms.

'Get creative with containers for your blooms: use old bottles, jars, tins, an old silver teapot, a vintage jug or a quirky ceramic pot from your local antiques market.'

Caroline Taylor, blogger

CHINESE INFLUENCE *Right* An oriental teapot decorated with cherry blossom and chirruping birds has been used to house a country garden collection of lupins and cow parsley against a backdrop of green. The result is perfect visual harmony.

GRASS VERGE *Below right* Claydies' award-winning Grass vase for Normann in Copenhagen is designed specifically to house the incidental flowers and hedgerow finds that you may often overlook in favour of something more sophisticated.

'For dressing up an elegant space, I love chartreuse, red and eggplant floral arrangements.' *Amy Atlas, event planner*

HOLDING THEIR OWN

Jugs, teapots, candle holders, bottles and jars are all good containers that double up as vases.

Vintage vases may have undetected cracks in them so check for leaks before you assemble a floral arrangement in a favourite flea market find.

If you have a beautiful container that is too damaged to hold water then use faux flowers instead.

Avoid using metal vases, as they can shorten a flower's lifespan.

Try to avoid using green brick floral foam, which is not biodegradable and causes flowers to dry out faster. It is also bound with formaldehyde, a know carcinogen. Bind stems with florist's wire instead.

Different flowers have different lifespans. Remove dead stems from mixed arrangements as they die to make the arrangement last the longest and look the freshest.

Have fun matching container to contents. Use a rustic jug for displaying bright peonies or place a natural collection of pods, berries and branches in a simple but curvy 1950s vase.

To show off a collection of interesting or colourful containers, place only a few flowers in each one so that they don't drag attention away from the main design story.

SHIMMERY ROSE *Opposite* Sania Pell filled a delicate fishbowl-shaped single-stem vase with tiny silver sequins to reflect the light in a glamorous rose-filled moment.

'I love using one large vase filled with flowers with a much smaller vase next to it with just one flower in it on my mantel. Keep adjusting positions until you are happy with the display. A good tip is to step back so you can see the overall display. Most of all, have fun with it.'

Selina Lake, stylist

BLUE HUES *This page* Blousy scabious blooms in blue are given the perfect emphasis by being placed in discarded jars and medicine bottles, bringing a hint of the herb garden to a windowsill.

TABLE SETTINGS

Use table settings to reflect your own personal style or create a celebratory mood for guests

'I use leftover fabric pieces as napkins and tablecloths – it's a clever and cheap way to re-use remnant fabric scraps and make your table one-of-a-kind.' *Tori Mellott, style witer*

Create a capsule collection of china in the same way as you would clothes in your wardrobe. A basic set of plain glassware can be used for everyday and in combination with interesting table cloths and a vase of jewel-bright flowers. Add in key pieces such as a vivid vase, colourful champagne flutes or wine glasses and rich-coloured napkins for a mix and match style that allows you to create a number of different looks using the same pieces.

PLAIN AND SIMPLE *Above left* By keeping the china plain you can have fun adding in linen mats and napkins for texture and colourful flowers to lift the neutral scene. Glassware can be textured, too.

LINEN PRESS *Above right* Linen napkins on earthenware plates resting on seagrass mats and embellished with a subtle butterfly theme are exquisitely set off by a jug of purple lilac on the table.

A FEMININE TOUCH Pink plates on a battered wooden table look beautifully delicate against hydrangea heads arranged in squat glass vases. Plain colourful china is good for any number of combinations at the table.

'Silverware and stemware needn't come from one set – in fact multiple styles and colours are more interesting and catch the attention of guests. Mini flower arrangements personalize the space and make a guest feel engaged.' *Matthew Mead, stylist*

SUMMER LUNCH Range several vases of flowers down a long table to create impact and a sense of luxury when entertaining. Guests always appreciate fresh flowers and a well-considered table setting as part of a strong sense of occasion.

'I have a slew of sturdy and good-looking white dinnerware for entertaining. I buy beautiful fresh flowers in bold and vibrant colours and let the food and the florals do the talking for me! Works like a charm every time.'

Tori Mellott, style writer

COLOURFUL CHINA Include candles
on the table and if they are in tall
candleholders, put small flower heads in
neat, low vases to vary the height of the
table decorations. If your china is plain,
go bold with blousy blooms to create
some visual intricacy.

'Use your good dinnerware and
serveware. Keep it accessible and
use it, not only for special occasions
but for when the mood strikes! It's
surprising what a mood-lifter it is to
use your good pieces.'

Susan Serra, kitchen designer

'Edit. Let go of things that don't make your heart sing. Purge. Get rid of anything that's cramping your style.'

Carrie McCarthy, author

'It is best to look for collections of an item – vases, paintings, busts. Creating a theme and displaying something en masse in your home can unify the space.'

Leslie Oschmann, designer

'I tell people that it's okay not to get it all done at once. Great design can be accumulated over time with editing and through trial and error. Your whims change. There is no silver bullet for designing a space of your own.'

Amy Butler, designer

'When mixing colours and patterns I will usually look for a colour that isn't the strongest in the pattern and I will look for a complementary pattern or colour that works well with it.' *Vivian Mansour, blogger*

'In my experience, there are two kinds of personalities when it comes to dealing with clutter: the spreaders and the pile makers. My husband is a spreader and I'm a pile maker. When I want to clear any sort of clutter, first I take everything my family has strewn all over every available surface and put it all into piles. Instantly I feel better. Instantly my surroundings look better. I can't explain it, but it feels like magic.' *Kristin van Ogtrop, editor in chief*

MIGHTY CHINA A delightful mix of Danish porcelain pieces forms a pleasing display of textural ceramics on top of a painted and distressed storage chest in the Copenhagen home of Mads Hagedorn-Olsen and his wife Karen Kjældgård-Larsen.

CONTRIBUTORS

Locations

We'd like to thank you, the talented and hospitable contributors, for opening your homes to share your unique and authentic personal space – your creativity and style impressed and inspired us and gave us many ideas to include in the text of this book. Your homes help make the photographs in this book so beautiful and for this we thank each one of you from the heart.

'I always recommend that a box of favourite things is put together for inspiration. People are attracted to the same colours and patterns over and over again in different combinations, often without even realizing it. These boxes can include anything from a favourite cocktail ring, book, dress, shells, found objects, invitations etc.'

Sibella Court, stylist

Jonathan Adler
Potter and Interior Designer
47 Greene Street
New York, NY 10013
+1 212 941 8950
www.jonathanadler.com
customerservice@jonathanadler.com
Simon Doonan
Creative Director of Barneys New York, writer, and author of the memoir
Beautiful People
www.barneys.com
www.simondoonan.net

Virginia Armstrong
Graphic and Textile Designer
Roddy & Ginger
London
www.roddyandginger.co.uk

Liz Bauer
Interior Designer/Shop Owner
Elizabeth Bauer Design
43 Greenwich Avenue
New York, NY 10014, USA
+1 212 255 8625
Liz@Elizabethbauerdesign.com
www.elizabethbauerdesign.com

Florienne Bosch
Hotel designer
Bed of Flowers
Dijk 45, 6651 LA Beuningen
Belgium
+31 24 6750849
www.bedofflowers.nl

Kristin Brandt
Creative Director
Bessermachen Design Studio
Copenhagen
+45 26450029
kb@bessermachen.com
www.bessermachen.com
Claus Spanner Elmholt
Artist
www.artsucker.com
Creative director
www.spinachagency.com

Sabine Brandt
Graphic Designer
Sisterbrant Design Studio
Oestergade 24 a, Copenhagen
sabine@sisterbrandt.dk
www.sisterbrandt.dk

Amy Butler
Designer
Amy Butler Design
122 S. Prospect St.
Granville OH 43023, USA
+1 740 587 2841
orders@amybutlerdesign.com
www.amybutlerdesign.com
David Butler
Photographer
Art of the Midwest
www.artofthemidwest.com

Lyndsay Caleo
Metalsmith/Designer
Fitzhugh Karol
Sculptor/Designer
www.fitzhughkarol.com
www.caleojewelry.com
www.thebrooklynhomecompany.com

Emily Chalmers
Stylist/Store Owner
Caravan
3 Redchurch Street
Shoreditch
London E2 7DJ
www.caravanstyle.com

Yvonne Eijkenduijn
Graphic Designer/Stylist
Lommel, Belgium
yvonne@yvestown.com
www.yvestown.com

Mairead Fanning
www.englishlocations.com
www.tefllab.co.uk

'Having a creative workspace at home is a simple luxury that anyone can (and should) have. Designate an area in your home as your "go-to" spot – it doesn't matter how big or small it is, just a place where you can sit down and be inspired.' *Jonathan Lo, editor/art director*

Charlotte Hedeman Gueniau
Owner
Philippe Gueniau
Creative Director
Rice
Havnegade 100 E
5000 Odense C
+45 63 11 35 35
rice@rice.dk
www.rice.dk

Thom Filicia
Interior Designer
info@thomfilicia.com
www.thomfilicia.com

Karen Kjældgård-Larsen
Ceramic Designer, Claydies
www.claydies.dk
Mads Hagedorn-Olsen
Photographer
www.hagedornhagen.com
www.morganmorell.com

Anita Kaushal
Stylist/Author
anita@anitakaushal.com
http://www.anitakaushal.com

Tine Kjeldsen
Owner/Creative Director
Tine K Home
Agerhatten 16
ADK-5220 Odense, Denmark
+45 45 66 01 02
www.tinekhome.dk

Rita Konig
Style Writer/Interior Designer
www.ritakonig.com

Gelaldine Larkin
Textile Designer
www.geraldinelarkin.com

Nathalie Lété
Artist/Author
+33 01 49 60 84 76
nathalie@nathalie-lete.com
www.nathalie-lete.com

Anna-Malin Lindgren
Blogger/Photographer/Illustrator
Helt Enkelt
Helsingborg, Sweden
www.heltenkelthosmig.blogspot.com

Frédéric Méchiche
Interior Designer
4 Rue Thorigny
75003 Paris, France
+33 1 42 78 78 28

Amy Neunsinger
Photographer/Co-Owner of cocodot
Shawn Gold
CEO of Cocodot
www.amyneunsinger.com
www.cocodot.com

Christine d'Ornano
International Vice President of cosmetic company Sisley
www.sisley-cosmetics.co.uk
www.sisley-cosmetics.com
Marzouk Al-Bader
Financier

Marc Palazzo
President
Melissa Palazzo
Creative Director
Pal + Smith
20321 Irvine Avenue, Building F
Newport Beach, CA 92707, USA
+1 888 725 7684
www.palandsmith.com

Alayne Patrick
Retail Store Owner/women's clothing wholesaler
Layla
86 Hoyt Street, Brooklyn, NY 11201-5819
+1 718 222 1933
info@layla-bklyn.com
www.layla-bklyn.com

Sania Pell
Stylist/Author
07977 125588
sania@misspell.co.uk
www.saniapell.com

Stephanie Rammeloo
Conceptual designer/writer/stylist
Dreamboat
stephaniesdreamboat.blogspot.com

Claus Robenhagen
Gallery Director, Galleri Nicolai Wallner
www.nicolaiwallner.com
Heidi Hofmann Møller
Senior Fashion Designer at Day Birger et Mikkelsen
www.day.dk

Leslie Shewring
Photographer/Stylist
A Creative Mint
www.acreativemint.typepad.com

Christina Strutt
Founder/Designer
Cabbages and Roses
3 Langton Street
London SW10 0JL
020 7352 7333
www.cabbagesandroses.com

Vicente Wolf
Interior Designer/Author
Vicente Wolf Associates
333 West 39th Street,
New York, NY 10018, USA
+1 212 465 0590
www.vicentewolf.com
www.vicentewolfblog.com

'The best rooms in a home are always painted white. So when the sun comes out your home is instantly the happiest place on earth.'
Yvonne Eijkenduijn, blogger

Picture Credits

Every effort has been made to trace the copyright holders, architects and designers. We apologize in advance for any unintentional omission and would be pleased to insert the appropriate acknowledgement in any subsequent edition.

All photographs were taken by Debi Treloar unless otherwise stated.

'When decorating for clients who are a little nervous of bold colour I usually suggest they do the larger upholstered pieces in a white or natural coloured linen and then add colour and pattern into the smaller pieces in the room. By doing this they can always change the cushions and accessory pieces if they tire of the patterns/colours we have selected.' *Anna Spiro, designer*

Photographer/Designers and locations

p1 Virginia Armstrong, London; p2-3 Sabine Brandt, Copenhagen; p4 Yvonne Eijkenduijn, Lommel, Belgium; p7 Amy Neunsinger, Los Angeles; p8-9 Virginia Armstrong, London; p10-11 Amy Neunsinger, Los Angeles; p13 Simon Upton/Frédéric Méchiche, Paris; p14-15 Lyndsay Caleo and Fitzhugh Karol, Brooklyn, NY; p17 Tine Kjeldsen, Rynkeby, Denmark; p18 above Sunil Vijayakar and Geraldine Larkin, London; p18 below Christine d'Ornano and Marzouk Al-Bader, London; p19 above Jonathan Adler and Simon Doonan, New York City; p19 below Vincent Knapp/Kelly Hoppen, London; p20 left Simon Upton/ Frédéric Méchiche, Paris; p20 right Simon Upton/ Frédérick Méchiche, Paris; p22-23 Marc and Melissa Palazzo, Orange County, CA; p24 David Butler /Amy & David Butler, Granville, Ohio; p25 Stephanie Rammeloo, Amsterdam; p26-9 Amy Neunsinger, Los Angeles; p30 above Anita Kaushal, London; p30 below Vicente Wolf, New York City; p31 Anita Kaushal, London; p32-5 Claus and Heidi Robenhagen, Copenhagen; p36 Frédéric Vasseur/Nathalie Lété, Paris; p37 Kristin Brandt and Claus Elmholt, Gentofte, Denmark; p38-41 Anna-Malin Lindgren, Helsingborg, Sweden; p42 left Mairead Fanning, London; p42 right Virginia Armstrong, London; p43 Mads Hagedorn-Olsen and Karen Kjældgård-Larsen, Copenhagen; p44 Marc and Melissa Palazzo, Orange County, CA; p45 Amy Neunsinger, Los Angeles; p46 Alayne Patrick, Brooklyn, NY; p47 Jonathan Adler and Simon Doonan, New York City; p48-51 Rita Konig, New York City; p52 Lyndsay Caleo and Fitzhugh Karol, Brooklyn, NY; p53 Marc and Melissa Palazzo, Orange County, CA; p54-7 Elizabeth Bauer, New York City; p58 Virginia Armstrong, London; p59 Tine Kjeldsen, Rynkeby, Denmark; p60 above left Amy Neunsinger, Los Angeles; p60 above right Charlotte Hedeman Gueniau, Kerteminde, Denmark; p60 below left Yvonne Eijkenduijn, Lommel, Belgium; p60 below right Christine d'Ornano and Marzouk Al-Bader, London; p61 Marc and Melissa Palazzo, Orange County, CA; p63 Virginia Armstrong, London; p64-5 Rita Konig, New York City; p66 mood board by Holly Becker; p67 Leslie Shewring, Rancho Palos Verdes, CA; p68-9, 71-3 mood boards by Holly Becker; p71-3 Leslie Shewring, Rancho Palos Verdes, CA; p74-81 Tine Kjeldsen, Rynkeby, Denmark; p82 Vicente Wolf, New York City, p83 top left Stephanie Rammeloo, Amsterdam; p83 above right Tine Kjeldsen, Rynkeby, Denmark; p83 below left Amy Neunsinger, Los Angeles; p83 below right

Anna-Malin Lindgren, Helsingborg, Sweden; p84-90 Lyndsay Caleo and Fitzhugh Karol, Brooklyn, NY, p91 above left Simon Upton/Alastair Gordon & Barbara de Vries, New Jersey; p91 above right Yvonne Eijkenduijn, Lommel, Belgium; p91 below left Anna-Malin Lindgren, Helsingborg, Sweden; p91 below right Simon Upton/Yvonne Sporre's house in London designed by J F Delsalle; p92-7 Virginia Armstrong, London, p98 David Butler /Amy & David Butler, Granville, Ohio; p99 above left Yvonne Eijkenduijn, Lommel, Belgium, p99 above right Virginia Armstrong, London; p99 below left Mairead Fanning, London; p99 below right Simon Upton/ Hanne Kjaerholm, Copenhagen; p100-4 Sania Pell, London; p106 Emily Chalmers, London; p107 above left Andrew Wood/Dominique Kieffer, Paris; p107 above right Kristin Brandt and Claus Elmholt, Gentofte, Denmark; p107 below left & right Kristin Brandt and Claus Elmholt, Gentofte, Denmark; p108-115 Alayne Patrick, Brooklyn, NY; p116 Yvonne Eijkenduijn, Lommel, Belgium; p117 Charlotte Hedeman Gueniau, Kerteminde, Denmark; p118 Alayne Patrick, Brooklyn, NY, p119 above left Yvonne Eijkenduijn, Lommel, Belgium; p119 above right Charlotte Hedeman Gueniau, Kerteminde, Denmark; p119 below right Anna-Malin Lindgren, Helsingborg, Sweden; p119 below right Mads Hagedorn-Olsen and Karen Kjældgård-Larsen, Copenhagen; p120 above Jonathan Adler and Simon Doonan, New York City; p120 below Virginia Armstrong, London; p121 above left Charlotte Hedeman Gueniau, Kerteminde, Denmark; p121 above right Virginia Armstrong, London; p121 below left Elizabeth Bauer, New York City, NY; p122 above Rita Konig, New York City, NY; p122 below Tine Kjeldsen, Rynkeby, Denmark; p123 above left Mads Hagedorn-Olsen and Karen Kjældgård-Larsen, Copenhagen; p123 below left Elizabeth Bauer, New York City; p123 below right - p129 Charlotte Hedeman Gueniau, Kerteminde, Denmark; p130 Yvonne Eijkenduijn, Lommel, Belgium; p131 above left Simon Upton/ Christina Strutt, Gloucestershire p131 top right Yvonne Eijkenduijn, Lommel, Belgium; p131 below left & right Simon Upton/Bed of Flowers, Netherlands designed by Floriene Bosch; p132-7 Jonathan Adler and Simon Doonan, New York City; p138-143 Marc and Melissa Palazzo, Orange County, CA; p145 Christine d'Ornano and Marzouk Al-Bader, London; p146-7 Mairead Fanning, London; p149 Sania Pell, London; p150 Yvonne Eijkenduijn, Lommel, Belgium; p151 left

'I love creating a sense of balance on a shelf or dresser, but it's tricky. When arranging things you always want to think about clustering them closer together rather than farther away from each other.' *Lisa Congdon, artist*

'I always display my collections in groupings of "like objects". If you can, for instance, keep all your white pottery organized in one display case – it creates a cohesive, smart look – rather than cluttering up your decor with your treasures scattered here and there around your home.'

Victoria Smith, blogger

Sources of Quotes

There are many who deserve thanks for helping make the vision behind *Decorate* come to fruition, from homeowners to those who provided helpful insights that we quoted throughout, listed below. Our international group of contributors were hand-picked based on their knowledge and professional accomplishments, though we regret we were not able to include all of the fantastic voices in the design world due to space limitations and deadlines. For those whom we have featured, from larger-than-life designers to extra stylish bloggers, thank you so much for being a part of this project — we are honoured to share your voice and expert advice in this book.

'Something unusual that no one else has is likely to be a great focal point. That thing can be a family heirloom, something kooky that makes you laugh or maybe something from your travels that has fond memories.'

Michele Varian, designer

Michelle Adams
Editor in Chief/Co-Founder of Lonny Magazine, Founder of Rubie Green
michelle.adams@rubiegreen.com
www.rubiegreen.com
www.lonnymag.com

Abigail Ahern
Designer/Shop Owner/Author
Atelier Abigail Ahern
137 Upper Street, London N1 1QP
020 7354 8181
contact@atelierbypost.com
www.atelierabigailahern.com

Rachel Ashwell
Interior Designer and Founder, Rachel Ashwell Shabby Chic Couture
202 Kensington Park Road,
London W11 1NR
info@chelashwellsshabbychiccouture.com
rachelashwellshabbychiccouture.com

Amy Atlas
Event and Sweets Stylist,
Amy Atlas Events, New York, NY
www.amyatlas.com
blog.amyatlas.com

Nicole Balch
Graphic Designer/Blogger, Pink Loves Brown and Making It Lovely
www.pinklovesbrown.com
www.makingitlovely.com

Atlanta Bartlett
Interior designer/stylist
Pale and Interesting
01797 344 077
www.paleandinteresting.com

Christina Batch-Lee
Partnerships Manager, Etsy
www.etsy.com

Nate Berkus
Interior Designer
The Nate Berkus Show/
Nate Berkus Associates
www.nateberkus.com
www.thenateshow.com/

Jane Brocket
Author
www.yarnstorm.blogs.com

Deborah Bibby
Editor in chief, Real Living magazine,
Australian Consolidated Press (ACP)
www.reallivingmag.com.au/

Pia Jane Bijkerk
Author/photographer/stylist
blog.piajanebijkerk.com

Fernanda Bourlot
Interior designer/store owner
Simplemente Blanco
460 Harrison ave. Building B, Gallery 15
Boston, MA 02118, USA
+1 617 734 3669
contactus@simplementeblanco.com
www.simplementeblanco.com

Betsy Burnham
Principal designer, Burnham Design
www.burnhamdesign.com
www.instantspacedesign.com

Emily Chalmers
Interior stylist, author and shop-owner
Caravan
3 Redchurch Street
Shoreditch, London E2 7DJ
www.caravanstyle.com

Lisa Congdon
Artist, designer and Illustrator
www.lisacongdon.com

Sibella Court
Stylist/Shopowner/author
The Society Inc.
www.thesocietyinc.com.au

Lulu deKwiatkowski
Founder and head designer, Lulu DK
www.luludk.com

Tom Delavan
Interior Designer/Owner, Tom Delavan
www.tomdelavan.com

Anna Dorfman
Graphic Designer/Blogger
Door Sixteen
www.doorsixteen.com

Emily Dyson
Owner,
Couverture
188 Kensington Park Road
Notting Hill, London W11 2ES
020 7229 2178
www.couverture.co.uk

Fired Earth
Twyford Mill, Oxford Road
Adderbury, Oxfordshire OX17 3SX
Head office 01295 814 399
Stockists 0845 366 0400
www.firedearth.com

Shannon Fricke
Interior Decorator/Stylist/Author
www.shannonfricke.com

Maxwell Gillingham-Ryan
Blogger, Interior Designer,
and Founder of Apartment Therapy
www.apartmenttherapy.com

Belinda Graham
Freelance Style Writer/Blogger
www.thehappyhomeblog.com

Gregory Han
Editor, Apartment Therapy
www.apartmenttherapy.com

Irene Hoofs
Author of lifestyle blogs Bloesem and B:Kids
bloesem.blogs.com
bkids.typepad.com

'Utilize harmonious colours to equalize even the most contrasting of designs when layering, while combining differing scale of patterns can impart a sophisticated depth to any room: big against small, simple with ornate, bright against monochromatic.' *Gregory Han, editor*

Lotta Jansdotter
Designer, Author and Founder
Lotta Jansdotter
119 8th Street #215
Brooklyn, NY 11215, USA
+1 718 596 2055
order@jansdotter.com
www.jansdotter.com

Niki Jones
Creative director of home accessories and furniture online store
Unit 13 D8
Anniesland Business Park
Netherton Road
Glasgow G13 1EU
0141 959 4090
www.niki-jones.co.uk

Celerie Kemble
Decorator, Kemble Interiors Inc
www.kembleinteriors.com

Selina Lake
Interior Stylist & Author
www.selinalake.co.uk
www.selinalake.blogspot.com

Kahi Lee
Interior designer and television personality
Kahi Lee Lifestyle
www.kahilee.com

Jenny Levié
Editor in Chief, Living at Home magazine, Gruner & Jahr
www.livingathome.de

Jonathan Lo
Editor/Art Director
www.j3productions.com
www.happymundane.com

Carrie McCarthy
Founder/Author, Style Statement
Live by Your Own Design
www.stylestatement.com

Vivian Mansour
Blogger, Ish and Chi
www.ishandchi.com

Matthew Mead
Creative Director/ Author
Matthew Mead Style
www.matthewmeadstyle.com

Tori Mellott
Freelance Editor and Stylist

Marie Nichols
Stylist
www.marienichols.co.uk

Claudia Nowotny
Store Owner/Theatre Designer
COMINGHOME Interior
Lindener Marktplatz 5
30449 Hannover, Germany
+49 11 2158196
www.cominghome-interior.de
info@cominghome-interior.de

Roger Oates
Textile Designer
1 Munro Terrace
Riley Street
London SW10 0DL
020 7351 2288
www.rogeroates.com

Kristin van Ogtrop
Managing editor, Real Simple magazine
www.realsimple.com

Leslie Oschmann
Artist/Designer
Swarm
www.swarmhome.com

Russell Pinch
Furniture Designer
Unit 1W
Clapham North Art Centre
26-32 Voltaire Road
London SW4 6DH
020 7622 5075
www.pinchdesign.com

Paula Pryke
Florist
Paula Pryke Flowers
The Flower House
Cynthia Street
London N1 9JF
020 7837 7336
www.paula-pryke-flowers.com

Jessie Randall
Creative Director, Loeffler Randall
www.loefflerrandall.com

Eddie Ross
Lifestyle Expert and Blogger
Eddie Ross, Inc.
www.eddieross.com

Danny Seo
Green Living Expert
www.dannyseo.com/

Susan Serra
Kitchen Designer and President, Susan Serra Associates, Inc.
www.kitcheninteriors.com
www.thekitchendesigner.org

Suzanne Sharp
Co-Founder and Creative Director
The Rug Company
124 Holland Park Avenue
London W11 4UE
020 7229 5148
www.therugcompany.info

Victoria Smith
Blogger, SFGirlByBay
www.sfgirlbybay.com

Ruthie Sommers
Interior Designer/owner
Chapman Radcliffe
www.ruthiesommers.com

Annette Tatum
Textile Designer/author
www.annettetatum.com

Anna Spiro
Interior designer/shop owner
Black & Spiro
www.blackandspiro.com.au

Caroline Taylor
UK blogger and online store owner
Patchwork Harmony
07985 174007
www.patchworkharmony.co.uk
patchworkharmony.blogspot.com

Michele Varian
Designer/ owner, Michele Varian
www.michelevarian.com
michelevarianblog.com

Vanessa de Vargas
Interior Designer, Turquoise
www.turquoise-la.com

Kelly Wearstler
Interior Designer/Owner
Kelly Wearstler Interior Design
760 North La Cienega Blvd
Los Angeles, CA 90069, USA
+1 323 951 7454
interior@kellywearstler.com
www.kellywearstler.com

Madeline Weinrib
Designer/Owner
Madeline Weinrib Atelier
contact@madelineweinrib.com
www.madelineweinrib.com

Marcia Zia-Priven
Design Director & CEO
Zia Priven, Inc.
7623, Fulton Avenue
N. Hollywood, CA 91605, USA
+1 818 765 2777
info@ziapriven.com
www.ziapriven.com

Pam Zsori
Owner
Ink & peat
Portland, Oregon
www.inkandpeat.com

DIRECTORY

GLASS + CERAMICS
From china meant for entertaining to a beloved plate for your morning toast, paying attention to the details is how your home can become a warm nest. Our selection of china, glass and ceramics show that function need not trump beauty.

Abode
01273 62116
www.abodeliving.co.uk
Contemporary Scandinavian vases and ceramics from Normann and Marimekko as well us UK designers.

Anne Black
+45 35 10 73 27
shoponline@anneblack.dk
www.shopanneblack.dk
Danish porcelain with a clean contemporary feel.

Annette Buganskyy
15 Camden Passage, London N1 8EA
www.loopknitting.com
Knitted textures form part of the pattern of these gorgeous pieces.

Anthropologie.com
+1 215 568 2114
020 3119 2907
www.anthropologie.com
A sensory shopping experience with unique ceramics and glassware carefully curated from around the world along with other household goods, furniture, fashion and accessories.

Astier de Villatte
173 rue Saint-Honoré
75001 Paris, France
+ 33 1 42 60 74 13
www.astierdevillate.com
Parisian store selling delicate handmade ceramics and tableware.

Bison
+61 2 6257 7255
info@bisonhome.com
www.bisonhome.com
Fine lead-free and food-safe durable stoneware from Australia.

Caroline Zoob
Anderton Works, Port Street
Middleport, Stoke-on-Trent
Staffordshire ST6 3PF
01782 826052
www.caroline-zoob.co.uk
Country style china collections.

Chinacraft Ltd
020 7565 5876
www.chinacraft.co.uk
Huge collection of UK and international tableware collections.

Clare Gage
The Studio, 479 Chatsworth Road
Chesterfield, Derbyshire S40 3AD
www.claregage.com
Award-winning designer of textile-inspired white ceramics.

The Conran Shop
Michelin House
81 Fulham Road
London SW3 6RD
0844 848 4000
www.conranshop.co.uk
Well considered contemporary china, glassware and tableware.

Contemporary Applied Arts
020 7436 2344
www.caa.org.uk
Charitable organization that promotes the best in contemporary British craft.

Danish Ceramics
+45 2680 3016
info@danishceramics.dk
www.danishceramics.com
Classic and experimental handmade ceramics.

Designers Guild
020 7893 7400
www.designersguild.com
Colourful porcelain, glass and ceramic tableware.

Design House Stockholm
020 7352 8403
www.designhousestockholm.com
Contemporary white and black tableware from Scandinavia.

Diana Fayt
+1 415 255 7045
diana@dianafayt.com
www.dianafayt.com
Clay platters, bowls and vases inspired by nature.

Dinosaur Designs
250 Mott Street
New York, NY 10012, USA
+1 212 680 3523
dinosaurny@earthlink.net
www.dinosaurdesigns.com.au
Maker of contemporary homewares and jewellery using resin, silver, glass and ceramics.

Divertimenti
227–229 Brompton Road
London SW3 2EP
020 7581 8065
www.divertimenti.co.uk
Cookware, tableware, kitchenware and glassware in a wide range of styles.

Far4
1020 First Avenue, Seattle, WA 98104, USA
+1 206 621 8831
info@far4.net
www.far4.net
Gorgeous collection of homewares; the fine ceramics and glassware in this shop really stand out the most.

Feinedinge
Krongasse 20 A-1050 Wien, Austria
+43 699 10 100 177
sandra@feinedinge.at
www.feinedinge.at
Austrian ceramicist who meticulously creates fine porcelain vases, cups and other wares (her lighting is enchanting).

Fishs Eddy
889 Broadway
New York, NY 10003, USA
+1 877 347 4733
www.fishseddy.com
Commercial quality dish and glassware.

The General Trading Company
020 7730 0411
www.general-trading.co.uk
Luxurious, high quality tableware and ceramics.

Heath Ceramics
+1 415 332 3732
www.heathceramics.com
One of the few remaining mid century potteries in America, each piece is made in their original factory in California.

House of Fraser
0844 800 3752
www.houseoffraser.co.uk
Dinnerware, glassware and china in a wide variety of styles.

Jan Burtz
sold exclusively at ABC Carpet & Home
888 Broadway
New York, NY 10003, USA
+1 212 473 3000
www.bellaporcelain.com
www.abchome.com
One-of-a-kind porcelain hand-crafted and glazed by artisan Jan Burtz.

Jane Hogben Terracotta
01753 882364
www.janehogbenterracotta.co.uk
Decorative terractotta pieces for the home and garden.

J. Mendicino
Earthworks Studio + Gallery,
2547 8th Street #33 Berkeley
CA 94710, USA
joanna@jmendicino.com
www.jmendicino.com
Crafty modern ceramics that are simple and clean (and may include birds and rabbits!).

John Lewis
08456 049 049
www.johnlewis.co.uk
Dinnerware, glassware and china in a wide variety of styles plus individual designers such as Sophie Conran for Portmeirion and Emma Bridgewater.

Jonathan Adler
47 Greene Street
New York, NY 10013, USA
+1 212 941 8950
www.jonathanadler.com
Potter Jonathan Adler mixes modernist forms with groovy graphics in bold colourways.

Karin Eriksson
+46 (0)8 655 11 60
info@karineriksson.se
www.karineriksson.se
Swedish designer who makes clean and simple vessels, tableware, one-off fine ceramic pieces.

Kathleen Hills
020 8293 0755
kathleen@kathleenhills.co.uk
www. kathleenhills.co.uk
Designer of simple, modern ceramic lighting and tableware.

Kosta Boda
+44 (0)0478 345 00
www.kostaboda.com
Classic Swedish contemporary glassware.

Kuehn Keramik
Fasanenstr. 58, 10719 Berlin, Germany
+ 49 30 28 384 695
info@kuehn-keramik.com
www.kuehn-keramik.com
German ceramics with vintage-inspired forms mixing with edgy motifs and cheeky words.

Lenneke Wispelwey
van oldenbarneveldtstraat 90-92
6827 AN Arnhem, The Netherlands
+31 (0)6 50 90 10 87
info@lennekewispelwey.nl
www.lennekewispelwey.nl
Dutch designed ceramics with a nod to the past and a playful edge.

Liberty
Regent Street
London W1B 5AH
020 7734 1234
www.liberty.co.uk
Wide range of Liberty print ceramics and designers such as Pip Studio, Thomas Hopkins Gibson, Nina Campbell and Rice.

Lovers of Blue & White
01763 853 800
www.blueandwhite.com
Antique and new blue and white china and pottery from UK producers such as Spode, Wedgwood, Masons and Davenport.

Moleta Munro
4 Jeffrey Street
Edinburgh EH1 1DT
0131 557 4800
www.moletamunro.com
Edinburgh store selling contemporary Scandinavian ceramics from Design House Stockholm, Hay, Muuto and Normann Copenhagen.

Molly Hatch
31 Lexington Avenue
Florence, MA 01062, USA
+1 413 896 5830
molly.hatch@yahoo.com
www.mollyhatch.com
Feminine patterns and forms with a modern feel inspired by fine French porcelain.

Mud
www.mudaustralia.com
Timeless, stylish and innovative ceramic homewares.

Nason Moretti
+ 390 41 7390 20
www.nasonmoretti.com
Contemporary Venetian glassware and tableware.

Nicole Farhi Home
17 Clifford Street
London W1S 3RQ
020 7494 9051
www.nicolefarhi.com
Decorative vases, glassware and
tableware in many colours and styles.

Petersham Nurseries
Church Lane, Off Petersham Road
Richmond, Surrey TW10 7AG
020 8940 5230
www.petershamnurseries.co.uk
French and Italian glassware and crockery
from Astier de Villatte and Nathalie Leté,
as well as terracotta tableware.

Pigeon Toe Ceramics
727 SE Morrison Street,
Portland, OR, USA
hello@pigeontoeceramics.com
www.pigeontoeceramics.com
Strong Scandinavian aesthetic – clean,
tactile, pure and white.

Rachel Dormor Ceramics
07771 9333948
www.racheldormorceramics.com
Beautiful handmade contemporary
porcelain tableware.

Rae Dunn
Fourth & Clay 2390 4th Street
Berkeley, CA 94710, USA
+1 415 515 9062
raedunn@aol.com
www.raedunn.com
Simple and playful ceramics inspired by
the Japanese aesthetic of wabi-sabi.

Royal Copenhagen
sales@royalcopenhagen.com
www.royalcopenhagen.com
Danish porcelain company founded in
1775 known for classic blue and white
floral motifs.

Royal Doulton
01782 404045
www.royaldoulton.com
Huge collection of tableware, crystal and
glassware.

R.Wood Studio
450 Georgia Drive,
Athens,GA 30605, USA
+1 888 817 9663
rwoodstudio@mindspring.com
www.rwoodstudio.com
Artists transform local red clay into simply
shaped and colourful ceramic dinnerware.

Sara Paloma
+1 510 701 5167
sara@sarapaloma.com
www.sarapaloma.com
Handcrafted pottery in soft whites made
in California.

Selfridges
400 Oxford Street
London W1A 1AB
020 7318 3779
www.selfridges.co.uk
Classic and contemporary tableware from
LSA, Royal Albert, Vera Wang, Michael
Aram and others.

Skandium
245–249 Brompton Road
London SW3 2EP
020 7224 2099
www.skandium.com
Scandinavian kitchen and tableware
from Stelton, Iitalla, Marimekko,
Tonfisk and other classic designers and
manufacturers.

Skujeniece
Krelis Louwenstraat 1 B29, 1055 KA
Amsterdam, The Netherlands
+31(0)6 502 777 95
mara@skujeniece.com
www.skujeniece.com
Vessels and plates handcrafted in the
Netherlands (furniture is made here too).

Spode
01782 744011
www.spode.com
Traditional British china and tableware.

Thomas Goode
19 South Audley Street
Mayfair, London W1K 2BN
www.thomasgoode.co.uk
020 7499 2823
Bespoke Thomas Goode luxury fine bone
china as well as Royal Copenhagen, KPM,
Herend and Paul Smith designs.

Up In The Air Somewhere
info@uptheairsomewhere.com
www.upintheairsomewhere.com
Drinkware, dishes, bowls and other wares,
some with elegant gold leafing and others
in organic shapes or with glossy glaze.

Vessel
114 Kensington park Road
London W11 2PW
020 7727 8001
www.vesselgallery.com
Prestigious glass and ceramic pieces
from a wide variety of international
craftspeople and designers.

Villeroy & Boch
020 8871 0011
www.villeroy-boch.com
Dinnerware and tableware in classic and
contemporary forms.

Wedgwood
01782 404045
www.wedgwood.com
Traditional classic ranges and
contemporary collections by Jasper
Conran, Vera Wang and Barbara Barry.

Wendy McLachlan Ceramics
+27 21 531 27 12
mail@homebakes.co.za
www.homebakes.co.za
Functional slip-cast range of 'teatime
ceramics and other delights'.

Whitney Smith Pottery
539 Athol Avenue,
Oakland, CA 94606, USA
+1 510 299 5936
whitney@whitneysmithpottery.com
www.whitneysmithpottery.com
Carefully hand carved and textured
ceramics inspired by nature.

FABRICS
From linens to faded florals,
embroidered cottons to silk, you can
find everything in this comprehensive
list to soften and personalize your
home.

Abbot & Boyd
020 7351 9985
www.abbottandboyd.co.uk

ABC Carpet & Home
888 Broadway
New York, NY 10083, USA
www.abchome.com

Amy Butler
122 S. Prospect Street
Granville OH 43023, USA
+1 740 587 2841
orders@amybutlerdesign.com
www.amybutlerdesign.com

Andrew Martin
020 7225 5100
+1 212 688 4498
www.andrewmartin.co.uk

Annette Tatum
1607 Montana Avenue
Santa Monica, CA 90403, USA
+1 310 451 1321
sales@annettetatum.com
www.annettetatum.com

Barbara Coupe
020 7720 1415
www.barbaracoupe.co.uk

Bholu
Suite 112, Level 1
59 Marlborough St, Surry Hills,
2010 NSW, Australia
+61 2 9698 0153
australia@bholu.com
www.bholu.com

Brunschwig & Fils
+1 914 872 1100
www.brunschwig.com

Cabbages and Roses
3 Langton Street
London SW10 0JL
020 7352 7333
ww.cabbagesandroses.com

Calico Corners
+1 800 213 6366
www.calicocorners.com

Camira Fabrics
01924 490591
www.camirafabrics.com

Cath Kidston
158 Portobello Road
London W11 2EB
08450 262 440
orderenquiries@cathkidston.co.uk
www.cathkidston.co.uk

Colefax & Fowler
110 Fulham Road
London SW3 6HU
020 7318 6000
www.colefax.com

Contempory Cloth
P.O. Box. 733, Willoughby, Ohio 44094-
0733, USA
+1 866 415 3372
sales@contemporarycloth.com
www.contemporarycloth.com

de le Cuona
01753 830301
www.delecuona.co.uk

Designers Guild
3 Latimer Place, London W10 6QT
020 7893 7400
info@designersguild.com
www.designersguild.com

Dominique Kieffer
+33 (0)1 42 21 32 44
www.dkieffer.com

Donghia
+1 212 925 2777
www.donghia.com

Duck Cloth
PO Box 100, Oakleigh South
VIC 3167, Australia
+61 3 8503 7615
info@duckcloth.com.au
www.duckcloth.com.au

DwellStudio
155 Sixth Ave, 7th Floor
New York, NY 10013, USA
+1 212 219 9343
customerservice@dwellstudio.com
www.dwellstudio.com

Florence Broadhurst
www.signatureprints.com.au

Flowie
contact@flowiestyle.com
www.flowiestyle.com

F. Schumacher & Co.
79 Madison Avenue, 15th Floor
New York, NY 10016, USA
+1 800-523-1200
info@fsco.com
www.fschumacher.com

G P & J Baker
020 7351 7760
www.gpjbaker.com

Grand Revival Design
+1 631 223 3323
+11 32 65 82 -4097
www. grandrevivaldesign.com
info@grandrevivaldesign.com

Hable Construction
The Old American Can Factory
232 3rd Street #E105
Brooklyn, NY 11215, USA
+1 718 834 1752
sales@hableconstruction.com
www.hableconstruction.com

Harlequin
08708 300032
www.harlequin.co.uk

Heather Bailey
4850 E. Baseline Rd. Suite 107
Mesa, AZ 85206, USA
+1 480 361 4275
customerservice@heatherbaileystore.com
www.heatherbaileystore.com

Henry Road
3949 Laurelgrove Avenue
Studio City, CA 91604, USA
+1 818 762 8966
info@henryroad.com
www.henryroad.com

Ian Mankin
020 7722 0997
www.ianmankin.co.uk

Jab Anstoetz
+ 49 0521 2093 0
JABverkauf@jab.de
www. jab.de

Joel Dewberry
113 West 1600
South Perry, Utah 84302, USA
+1 435 730 2399
joel@joeldewberry.com
www.joeldewberry.com

John Derian Dry Goods
10 East Second Street
New York, NY 10003, USA
+1 212 677 8408
drygoods@johnderian.com
www.johnderian.com

John Lewis
08456 049 049
www.johnlewis.com

John Robshaw Textiles
245 West 29th St., Suite 1501
New York, NY 10001, USA
+1 212 594 6006
info@johnrobshaw.com
www.johnrobshaw.com

Just Scandinavian
161 Hudson Street
New York, NY 10013, USA
+1 212 334-2556
info@justscandinavian.com
www.justscandinavian.com

Kalla Design
3408 Kayo
Shimotsuma-shi
Ibaraki 304-0048, Japan
+81 80 1163 8961
studio@kalladesign.com
www.kalladesign.com

Kathryn Ireland Fabrics
+1 310 246 1906
020 7751 4554
www.kathrynireland.com

Kelly Hoppen Interiors
102a Chepstow Road
St Stephen's Yard
London W2 5QW
020 7471 3350
www.kellyhoppen.com

Kerry Cassill
1145 South Coast Highway
Laguna Beach, CA 92651, USA
+1 949 497 4422
sales@kerrycassill.com
www.kerrycassill.com

Kravet
225 Central Avenue South
Bethpage, NY 11714, USA
+1 516 293 2000
customer.service@kravet.com
www.kravet.com

Layla
86 Hoyt Street
Brooklyn, NY 11201, USA
+1 718 222 1933
info@layla-bklyn.com
www.layla-bklyn.com

Lee Jofa
201 Central Ave South
Bethpage, NY 11714, USA
+1 800 453 3563
customer.service@leejofa.com
www.leejofa.com

Lena Corwin
info@lenacorwin.com
www.lenacorwin.com

Lisa Stickley
74 Landor Road
London SW9 9PH
020 7737 8067
www.lisastickleylondon.com

Lotta Jansdotter
119 8th Street #215
Brooklyn, NY 11215, USA
+1 718 596 2055
order@jansdotter.com
www.jansdotter.com

Malabar
020 7501 4200
+1 877 625 2227
www.malabar.co.uk

Marimekko
1262 Third Avenue
New York, NY 10021, USA
+1 800 527 0624
info@kiitosmarimekko.com
www.kiitosmarimekko.com

Mod Green Pod
1507 W. Koenig Lane
Austin, TX 78756, USA
+1 512 524 5196
info@modgreenpod.com
www.modgreenpod.com

Modern Fabrics
128 East Park Avenue
Charlotte, NC 28203, USA
+1 704 740 9675
service@modern-fabrics.com
www.modern-fabrics.com

Niki Jones
Unit 13 D8, Anniesland Business Park
Netherton Road
Glasgow G13 1EU
0141 959 4090
www.niki-jones.co.uk

Nina Campbell
9 Walton Street
London SW3 2JD
020 7225 1011
www.ninacampbell.com

Orla Kiely
31 Monmouth Street
London WC2H 9DD
020 7720 1117
www.orlakiely.com

Osborne & Little
304 King's Road
London SW3 5UH
020 7352 1456
+1 212 751 3333
www.osborneandlittle.com

Publisher Textiles
Unit 1/87 Moore Street
Leichhardt, Sydney, NSW
2040,Australia
info@publishertextiles.com.au
+61 2 9569 6044
www.publishertextiles.com.au

Purl Soho
459 Broome Street
New York, NY 10013, USA
+1 212 420 8796
customerservice@purlsoho.com
www.purlsoho.com

Rachel Ashwell Shabby Chic Couture
202 Kensington Park Road,
London W11 1NR
info@rachelashwellshabbychiccouture.com
www.rachelashwellshabbychiccouture.com

Robert Allen Design
225 Foxboro Boulevard
Foxboro, MA 02035, USA
+1 800 333 3777
www.robertallendesign.com

Robert Allen Design
Chiltern House
The Valley Centre
Gordon Road, High Wycombe
Buckinghamshire HP13 6EQ
01494 474741
www.robertallendesign.com

Roddy & Ginger
www.roddyandginger.co.uk

Roger Oates Design
1 Munro Terrace, Riley Street
London SW10 0DL
020 7351 2288
www.rogeroates.com

Romo
01623 756699
www.romo.om

Rubie Green
michelle.adams@rubiegreen.com
www.rubiegreen.com

St Judes
Wolterton Road
Itteringham, Norfolk NR11 7AF
01263 587666
www.stjudes.co.uk

Sanderson
01895 830044
+1 800 894 6185
www.sanderson-uk.com

Simrin # 10 Jay Street Suite 507
Brooklyn, NY 11201, USA
+1 718 797 8758
sylvia@simrininc.com
www.simrininc.com

Skinny LaMinx
Cape Town, South Africa
www.skinnylaminx.info

Spoonflower
2810 Meridian Parkway, Suite 130
Durham, NC 27713, USA
+1 919 321 2949
www.spoonflower.com

Sunbrella
1831 North Park Avenue
Glen Raven, NC 27217-1100, USA
+1 336 221 2211
www.sunbrella.com

Textile Arts
PO Box 3151, Sag Harbor
NY 11963, USA
+1 888-343-7285
info@txtlart.com
www.txtlart.com

Three Sheets 2 the Wind
info@threesheets2.com
www.threesheets2.com

Twins' Garden
Auguststr 67
D-26121 Oldenburg, Germany
+49 044 1 1 98 330 610
info@twinsgarden.de
www.twinsgarden.de

Virginia Johnson
132 Ossington Avenue
Toronto, ON M6J 2Z5 Canada
+1 416 516 3366
info@virginiajohnson.com
www.virginiajohnson.com

Volksfaden
Teutonenstr.1
14129 Berlin, Germany
+49 (0)30 72297057
info@volksfaden.de
www.volksfaden.de

FLOWERS
Flowers bring the outside in and add colour, texture and fragrance to a room that instantly wakes it up and makes the home feel welcoming and alive. Start with your local florist, farmers' market or flea market for fresh flowers, or seek out the incredibly realistic new faux designs.

Air Plant Supply Co. (Plants)
+1 312 608 2486
info@airplantsupplyco.com
www.airplantsupplyco.com

Atelier Abigail Ahern (Faux)
137 Upper Street, London N1 1QP
020 7354 8181
contact@atelierbypost.com
www.atelierabigailahern.com

Belmont Flower Market
2558 North Clark Street
Chicago, IL 60614, USA
+1 773 529 8770

Bloom (Faux)
0844 482 23332
www.bloom.uk.com

California Farmers' Market Association
830 Navaronne Way
Concord, CA 94518, USA
+1 800 806 94518
www.cafarmersmarkets.com

Chelsea Flower Market
75 9th Ave New York, NY 10011, USA
+1 212 620 7500

Fleurop Worldwide Florist
www.fleurop.com

Flower Wild
Los Angeles, California, USA
+1 818 729 0309
info@flowerwild.com
www.flowerwild.com

Greenmarket
Grow NYC
51 Chambers Street, Room 228
New York, NY 10007, USA
+1 212 788 7476
www.grownyc.org/greenmarket

Greenware Design (Plants)
www.greenwaredesign.etsy.com

Home Depot
www.homedepot.com

Horchow (Faux)
www.horchow.com

Ink & Peat
3808 N. Williams Avenue
Portland, OR 97227, USA
+1 503 282 6688
info@inkandpeat.com
www.inkandpeat.com

Interflora
0844 453 5600
www.interflora.co.uk

Jane Packer
020 7935 2673
www.jane-packer.co.uk

John Lewis
08456 049 049
www.johnlewis.co.uk

Los Angeles Flower Market
766 Wall Street
Los Angeles, California, USA
+1 213 622 1966
www.LAFlowerDistrict.com

Marks & Spencer
www.marksandspencer.com

Michael's Craft Store (Faux)
www.michaels.com

Moyses Stevens
020 8772 0094
www.moysesflowers.co.uk

Nikki Tibbles Wild at Heart
020 7229 1174
www.wildatheart.com

Peony (Faux)
service@peonydirect.co.uk
www.peony.co.uk

Paula Pryke Flowers
The Flower House
Cynthia Street
London N1 9JF
020 7837 7336
www.paula-pryke-flowers.com

Rosenow Floral Design
San Francisco, CA, USA
+1 415 424 7437
rosenowfloral@gmail.com
www.rosenowfloral.com

Martha Stewart Flowers
1-800-4-MARTHA
www.shop.marthastewart.com

Saipua
147 Van Dyke Street
Brooklyn, NY 11231, USA
+1 718 624 2929
www.saipua.com

Sylvia Hague (Faux)
www.sylviahague.com

Teleflora
www.teleflora.com

Terrain at Styer's
914 Baltimore Pike
Glen Mills, PA 19342, USA
+1 610 459 2400
TerrainatHome@TerrainatHome.com
www.styers.shopterrain.com

Whole Foods Market
www.wholefoodsmarket.com

Winston Flowers
Boston, MA, USA
1 800 457 4901
www.winstonflowers.com

FURNITURE
Do you like contemporary? French country? Mid-century modern? Here are some favourites for good design that will fit any budget and style.

ABC Carpet & Home
www.abchome.com

Alfies Antique Market
13–25 Church Street
London NW8 8DT
020 7723 6066
www.alfiesantiques.com

Anthropologie
info@anthropologie.eu
www.anthropologie.com

Artvoll
+49 (0) 30 86200277
www.artvoll.de

Baileys Home & Garden
Whitecross Farm
Bridstow HR9 6JU
01989 561931
www.baileyshomeandgarden.com

Barneys New York
+1 212 826 8900
www.barneys.com

Benchmark Furniture
Bath Road, Kintbury
Hungerford, Berkshire RG17 9SA
01488 658184
www.benchmarkfurniture.com

Bodie and Fou
020 8450 5600
www.bodieandfou.com

Camel and Yak
47a Bell Street
Reigate, Surrey RH2 7AQ
01737 222 441
www.camelandyak.co.uk

Car Moebel
T. Küstermann e. K.
Gutenbergstrasse 9 a
24558 Henstedt-Ulzburg
Germany
+49 04193 75 55 0
office@car-moebel.de
www. car-moebel.de

Catherine Memmi
11 rue Saint Sulphice
75006 Paris, France
+33 1 44 07 02 02
www.catherinememmi.com

CB2
+1 800 606 6252
www. cb2.com

Century
58 Blandford Street
London W1U 7JB
020 7487 5100
shop@centuryd.com

The Conran Shop
Michelin House, 81 Fulham Road
London SW3 6RD
020 7589 7401
407 East 59th Street, New York,
NY 10022, USA
+1 212 755 9079
orders@conran.com
www.conran.com

Corporate Culture
21–23 Levey Street
Chippendale NSW 2008, Australia
+ 61 2 9690 0077
info@corporateculture.com.au
www.corporateculture.com.au

Couverture
188 Kensington Park Road
London W11 2ES
020 7229 2178
www.couverture.co.uk

Crate & Barrel
+ 1 800 967 6696
www.crateandbarrel.com

Danish Furniture Design
+ 45 22 44 66 66
info@danishfurnituredesign.com
www.danishfurnituredesign.com

Dedece
263 Liverpool Street, Darlinghurst
Sydney 2010, Australia
+61 2 9360 2722
john@dedece.com
www.dedece.com

Designers Guild
3 Latimer Place
London W10 6QT
0207 893 7400
info@designersguild.com
www.designersguild.com

Domayne
www.domayne.com.au

Elizabeth Bauer Design
43 Greenwich Avenue
New York, NY 10014, USA
+1 212 255 8625
Liz@Elizabethbauerdesign.com
www.elizabethbauerdesign.com

George Smith Sofas
www.georgesmith.co.uk

Habitat
0844 499 4686
onlineservices@habitat.co.uk
www.habitat.co.uk

Heal's
The Heal's Building
196 Tottenham Court Road
London W1T 7LQ
08700 240 780
www.heals.co.uk

Heine
Heinrich Heine GmbH
Stephanie Lerch
76115 Karlsruhe, Germany
+61 0180 536 36
service@heine.de
www.heine.de

Homegoods
+1 800 614 4663
www.homegoods.com

House Doctor
Industrivej 29
DK-7430 Ikast, Denmark
+45 97 25 27 14
www.housedoctor.dk

IKEA
08453 583 363
www.ikea.co.uk
www.ikea.com

Impressionen
D - 22877 Wedel
+ 61 180 523 23 41
www.impressionen.de

John Lewis
08456 049 049
www.johnlewis.com

Jonathan Adler
customerservice@jonathanadler.com
www.jonathanadler.com

King
+ 61 1300 546 43876 48873
info@kingfurniture.com.au
www.kingfurniture.com.au

Laura Ashley
0871 983 5999
www.lauraashley.com

Liberty
Regent Street
London W1B 5AH
020 7734 1234
www.liberty.co.uk

Merci
111 Boulevard Beaumarchais 75003
Paris, France
+33 1 42 77 00 33
www.merci-merci.com

Mitchell Gold + Bob Williams
www.mgbwhome.com

Moooi
Minervum 7003, 4817 ZL Breda, PO
Box 5703
4801 EC Breda, The Netherlands
+ 0031(0) 76 578 4444
info@mooi.com
www.moooi.com

Nest
0114 24330000
www.nest.co.uk

Objx
Studio 3B/9 Chester Street
Fortitude Valley, Queensland 4006,
Australia
+61 7 32521633
info@objx.com.au
www.objx.com.au

Ochre
Studio G20 Clerkenwell Workshops
27/31 Clerkenwell Close
London EC1R 0AT
020 7096 7372 |
enquiries@ochre.net
www.ochre.net

OKA
01865 342 300
www.okadirect.com

Pal + Smith
20321 Irvine Avenue, Building F
Newport Beach, CA 92707
888 725 7684
www.palandsmith.com

Piet Boon
Ambacht 6, 1511 JZ Oostzaan,
The Netherlands
+31 (0)75 655 90 01
info@pietboon.com
www.pietboon.com

Pinch Design
Unit 1W, Clapham North Art Centre
26–32 Voltaire Road, London SW4 6DH
020 7622 5075
www.pinchdesign.com

Pottery Barn
+1 888 779 5176
www.potterybarn.com

Propeller
555 Hayes Street
San Francisco CA 94102, USA
+1 415 701 7728
contact@propellermodern.com
www.propellermodern.com

Purves & Purves
020 8893 4000
www.purves.co.uk

Robert Widmann
Briennerstr. 48
80333 Munich, Germany
+49(0)8954243624
einrichtungen@robertwidmann.de
www.robertwidmann.de

Room & Board
+1 800 301 9720
www.roomandboard.com

Rose & Grey
The Basement, 51 Ashfield Road
Altrincham, Cheshire WA15 9QJ
0560 311 3405
www.roseandgrey.co.uk

Sasha Waddell Furniture
020 8979 9189
www. sashawaddell.co.uk

Selfridges
400 Oxford Street
London W1S 1AB
0800 123 400
www.selfridges.com

Shabby Chic Couture
info@rachelashwellsshabbychiccouture.
com
www.rachelashwellsshabbychiccouture.
com

Space Furniture
infosydney@spacefurniture.com.au
www.spacefurniture.com.au

Squint
178 Shoreditch High Street
London E1 6HU
020 7739 9275
www.squintllimited.com

Twentytwentyone
020 7288 1996
www.twentytwentyone.com

Ute
PO Box 6102, West Footscray
Victoria 3012, Australia
+61 0417 562 250
info@ute.net.au
www.ute.net.au

West Elm
+ 1 888 922 4119
customerservice@westelm.com
www.westelm.com

Z Gallerie
+1 800 908 6748
customerservice@zgallerie.com
www.zgallerie.com

LIGHTING
Pendants, floor lights, sconces –
carefully selected lighting can create
the perfect mood for either a cosy
reading nook or a magical dinner party.

2Modern (online)
+1 888 222 4410
www.2modern.com

Artemide
+44 (0) 207 631 5200
www.artimede.com

Ascolights
0845 2600 268
www.ascolights.co.uk

Atelier Abigail Ahern
137 Upper Street
London NI IQP
0207 354 8181
www.atelierabigailahern.com
contact@atelierbypost.com

B & Q
0845 609 6688
www.diy.com

Baileys Home & Garden
Whitecross Farm
Bridstow HR96JU
01989 561931
www.baileyshomeandgarden.com

BHS
0845 196 0000
www.bhs.co.uk

Bleu Nature
26 rue Favreuil
59100 Roubaix, France
0033(0) 320 11 25 28
contact@bleunature.com
www.bleunature.com

Bock Lighting (online)
30901 Carter Street
Solon, Ohio 44139 USA
+1 216 912 7050
sales@bocklighting.com
www.bocklighting.com

Brabin & Fitz
01244 349 756
www.brabinandfitz.co.uk

Bruce Monro Ltd
Long Knoll Barns, Cokers Lane
Kilmington, Warminster
Wiltshire BA12 7HU
01985 845 228
www.brucemonro.co.uk

Caravan
3 Redchurch Street
London E2 7DJ
020 7033 3532
info@caravanstyle.com
www.caravanstyle.com

Casper Slieker
020 7751 5577
www.casperslieker.com

Chelsea Lighting Design Ltd
Unit 1, 23a Smith Street
London SW3 4EJ
020 7824 8144
www.chelsealightingdesign.co.uk

Christopher Wray Limited
591–93 King's Road
London SW6 2YW
020 7751 8701
www.christopherwray.com

C.S. Post & Co.
211 West Mill Street
Plainville, KS, USA
+1 888 419 2399
info@cspost.com
www.cspost.com

David Atkinson Lighting Design Ltd
13 Palace Road, Hampton Court
Surrey KT8 9DJ
020 8979 6113
www.dald.co.uk

Design Within Reach
1 Montgomery St, 2nd Floor
San Francisco, CA 94104, USA
1 800 944 2233
www.dwr.com

Dominic Myott Lighting
0143871 8226
www.greatlights.co.uk

Eden & Eden
560 Jackson Street
San Francisco, CA 94133, USA
+1 415 983 0490
hello@edenandeden.com
www.edenandeden.com

Foundry Light + Design
020 7232 4710
www.foundryonline.co.uk

The Future Perfect
+1 877 388 7373
hello@thefutureperfect.com
www.thefutureperfect.com

Gordon Watson
28 Pimlico Road
London SW1W 8LJ
020 7259 0555
www.gordonwatson.co.uk

Gracious Home
1220 Third Avenue
New York, NY 10021, USA
info@gracioushome.com
www.gracioushome.com

Habitat
0844 499 1111
www.habitat.co.uk

Heals
196 Tottenham Court Rd
London W1T 7LQ
08700 230 780
www.heals.co.uk

Hogarth Lighting
0800 328 8051
www.hogarthlighting.co.uk

Hunkydory Home
0191 645 4004
www.hunkydoryhome.co.uk

IKEA
08453 583 363
www.ikea.co.uk
www.ikea.com

Jayson Home & Garden
1885 North Clybourn Ave
Chicago, IL 60614, USA
+1 773 248 8180
info@jaysonhome.com
www.jaysonhomeandgarden.com

Jim Lawrence
01473 826685
www.jim-lawrence.co.uk

John Cullen Lighting
561–563 King's Road
London SW6 2EB
020 7371 5400
www.johncullenlighting.co.uk

John Lewis
08456 049 049
www.johnlewis.co.uk

Jonathan Adler
+ 1 800 963 0891
customerservice@jonathanadler.com
www.jonathanadler.com

Kate Beard Lighting
124 Hammersmith Grove
London W6 7HB
020 8222 8638
www.katebearlighting.com

Lahumiere
+ 33 06 86 27 77 97
www.lahumieredesign.fr

Liberty
Regent Street
London W1B 5AH
020 7734 1234
londonstorecustomerservices@liberty.
co.uk
www.liberty.co.uk

Lights Up!
2932 Fulton Street
Brooklyn, NY 11207, USA
+1 718 513 3770
www.lightsup.info

Lindsey Adelman
55 Great Jones Street
New York, NY 10012, USA
+1 212 473 2501
info@lindseyadelman.com
www.lindseyadelman.com

Lotus Bleu
325 Hayes Street
San Francisco CA 94102, USA
www.lotusbleudesign.com

Miljo
23C Curlewis Street
Bondi Beach, Australia
info@miljoshop.com
www.miljoshop.com
+61 02 9130 6445

Modernica
7366 Beverly Blvd
Los Angeles, CA 90036, USA
+1 323 933 0383
info@modernica.net
www.modernica.net

Moooi
Westerstraat 187
1015 MA Amsterdam
The Netherlands
0031 (0)20 5287760
info@moooi-gallery.com
www.moooi.com

Moth Design
+1 213 221 7277
sales@mothdesign.com
www.mothdesign.com

Neena's Lighting
+ 1 888 995 2677
www.neenaslighting.com

Normann Copenhagen
Osterbrogade 70
2100 Copenhagen, Denmark
+45 35 55 44 59
shop@normann-copenhagen.com
www.normann-copenhagen.com

Ochre
020 7096 7372
www.ochre.net

Omega Too
2204 San Pablo Avenue
Berkeley, CA 94702, USA
+1 510 843 3636
www.omegatoo.com

Orike Muth
Weberstraße 26
30449 Hannover, Germany
+0049 0511 452560
team@orikemuth.de
www.orikemuth.de

Patrick Townsend
50-17 5th Street
Long Island City, NY 11101, USA
+1 718 706 6462
ptownsend@erols.com
www.townsenddesign.net

Paper Cloud
1403 Central Parkway #204
Cincinnati, OH 45214, USA
+1 513 221 2862
contact@paper-cloud.com
www.paper-cloud.com

Perch!
201 Richards St. #7
Brooklyn, NY 11231, USA
+1 718 858 9399
info@perchceramics.com
www.perchdesign.net

Pols Potten
KNSM-laan 39
1019 LA Amsterdam, The Netherlands
+31 (0)20 4193541
winkel@polspotten.nl
www.polspotten.nl

Rockett St George
020 8350 5450
contact@rockettstgeorge.co.uk
www.rockettstgeorge.co.uk

Shades of Light (online)
4924 West Broad Street
Richmond, VA 23230, USA
+ 1 800 262 6612
cservice@shadesoflight.com
www.shadesoflight.com

Skinflint Design
5 Windsor Terrace, Falmouth
Cornwall TR11 3BP
01326 314528
www.skinflintdesign.co.uk

Spina Design
Kingsgate Place
London NW6 4TA
020 7328 5274
www.spinadesign.co.uk

Studio Tord Boontje
Unit 308, 30 Great Guildford Street
London SE1 0HS
020 3142 6220
info@tordboontje.com
www.tordboontje.com

Thomas Paul
info@thomaspaul.com
www.thomaspaul.com

Velocity Art & Design
251 Yale Ave N.
Seattle, WA 98109, USA
+1 206 749 9575
www.velocityartanddesign.com

Vaughan
D & D Building Suite 1511, 979 Third
Avenue
New York NY 10022, USA
+1 212 319 7070
us-sales@vaughandesigns.com
www.vaughandesigns.com

W Sitch & Company Ltd
48 Berwick Street
London W1F 8JD
020 7437 3776
www.wsitch.co.uk

Y Lighting
+1 866 428 9289
alexis@ylighting.com
www.ylighting.com

Zia Priven
7623 Fulton Avenue
N. Hollywood, CA 91605, USA
+1 818 765 2777
info@ziapriven.com
www.ziapriven.com

ONLINE HANDMADE MARKETS
Handmade art and crafts need not be kitschy – unless you want them to be! Here are some terrific places to start as you begin searching for unique finds that are not mass-produced but made with love. Support both emerging and established independent artists and designers, from ceramicists to textile artists and lighting designers, by shopping from them in these vibrant online marketplaces.

DaWanda
+44 20 30140720
feedback-en@dawanda.com
www.en.dawanda.com

Etsy
support@etsy.com
www.etsy.com

Folksy
be@folksy.com
www.folksy.com

Made It
83 428 672 923
sales@madeit.com.au
www.madeit.com.au

Robin Street Market
customerservice@robinstreetmarket.
com
www.robinstreetmarket.com

Supermarket
hello@supermarkethq.com
www.supermarkethq.com

PAINT
Unbeatable paints from some of the best, including eco-choices such as milk paint. It's amazing what a fresh coat of color can do for a room or a piece of furniture!

(Eco) indicates suppliers of eco friendly, natural or low VOC paints.

Auro Natural Paints (Eco)
Cheltenham Road, Bisley
Nr Stroud, Gloucestershire GL6 7BX
01452 772020
sales@auro.co.uk
www. auro.co.uk

Benjamin Moore
101 Paragon Drive,
Montvale NJ 07645, USA
info@benjaminmoore.com
www.benjaminmoore.com

Behr
3400 W. Segerstrom Ave., Santa Ana,
CA 92704, USA
714 545 7101
www.behr.com

California Paints
150 Dascomb Road, Andover, MA
01810, USA
1 800 225 1141
info@californiapaints.com
www. californiapaints.com

Craig & Rose
Unit 8m, Halbeath Industrial Estate
Dunfermline
Fife KY11 7EG
01383 740011
www.craigandrose.com

Crown Paints
0870 2401127
www.crownpaint.co.uk

Designers Guild
020 7893 7400
www.designersguild.com

Dulux Paints
Slough, UK
08444 817 817
www.dulux.co.uk

ECOS Organic Paints *(Eco)*
Unit 19, Heysham Business Park
Middleton Road, Heysham
Lancs LA3 3PP
01524 852371
www.ecospaints.com

Farrow & Ball
Uddens Estate, Wimborne
Dorset BH21 7NL
01202 876141
www.farrow-ball.com

Fired Earth
Twyford Mill, Oxford Road
Adderbury, Oxfordshire OX17 3SX
Head office 01295 814 399
Stockists 0845 366 0400
www.firedearth.com

Flamant
The Original Paint Collection
p/a Dendermondseseteenweg 75
B-9300 Aalst, Belgium
+32 53 76 80 21
www.flamantpaint.com

Francesca's Paints *(Eco)*
Unit 34, Battersea Business Centre
99/10 Lavender Hill
London SW11 5QL
020 7228 7694
www.francescapaint.com

The Freshaire Choice *(Eco)*
Available exclusively at Home Depot
+1 866 880 0304
freshairechoice@akzonobel.com
www.freshairechoice.com

Glidden
+1 800 454 3336
www.glidden.com

Kelly Hoppen Interiors
102a Chepstow Road
St Stephen's Yard
London W2 5QW
020 7471 3350
www.kellyhoppen.com

The Little Greene Paint Company *(Eco)*
Wood Street, Openshaw
Manchester M11 2FP
0845 880 5855
www.thelittlegreene.com

Kelly Moore
987 Commercial Street,
San Carlos, CA 94070, USA
+1 800 874 4436
www.kellymoore.com

Mythic Paint *(Eco)*
2714 Hardy Street Hattiesburg, MS
39401, USA
+1 888 714 9422
info@mythicpaint.com
www.mythicpaint.com

Nutshell Natural Paints *(Eco)*
Unit 3, Leigham Units
Silverton Road, Matford Park
Exeter, Devon EX2 8HY
01392 823760
www.nutshellpaints.com

The Old Fashioned Milk Paint Co., Inc.
(Eco)
436 Main Street,
Groton, MA 01450, USA
+1 978 448 6336
questions@milkpaint.com
www.milkpaint.com

Olympic One
PPG Place, Pittsburgh, PA 15272, USA
+1 800 441 9695
tchsrvaf@ppg.com
www.olympic.com

The Paint & Paper Library
5 Elystan Street
London SW3 3NT
020 7590 9860
www.paintlibrary.co.uk

Papers & Paints
4 Park Walk
London SW10 0AD
020 7352 8626
www.papers-paints.co.uk

Pittsburg Paints
One PPG Place, Pittsburgh,
PA 15272, USA
+1 800 441 9695
tchsrvaf@ppg.com
www.ppgpittsburghpaints.com

Pratt & Lambert
+1 800 289 7728
www.prattandlambert.com

Sanderson
0844 543 4749
www.sanderson-uk.com

The Sherwin-Williams Company
www.sherwin-williams.com

The Society Inc.
Exclusively for Murobond Paints
81 Dickson Avenue, Artarmon NSW
2064, Australia
1 800 199 299
www. murobond.com.au

Martha Stewart Living Paint
Exclusively available at Home Depot
+ 1 800 466 3337
www.homedepot.com

Valspar
8725 West Higgins Road, Suite 1000,
Chicago, IL 60631-2716, USA
+1 800 845 9061
www.valspar.com

Yolo Colorhouse (Eco)
www. yolocolorhouse.com
info@yolocolorhouse.com

RUGS
Nothing beats the warmth and beauty
of a gorgeous rug. Sisal, jute, plush,
flat weave – take your pick . . . and see
where your magic carpet takes you.

Angela Adams
273 Congress Street
Portland, Maine 04101, USA
+ 1 207 774 3523
customerservice@angelaadams.com
www.angelaadams.com

Jonathan Adler
+ 1 800 963 0891
customerservice@jonathanadler.com
www.jonathanadler.com/rugs

Ballard Designs
+ 1 800 367 2775
customerservice@ballarddesigns.net
www.ballarddesigns.com

Nina Burgess Carpets & Rugs
020 7731 4191
www.ninaburgess.co.uk

Christopher Farr
6 Burnsall Street
London SW3 3ST
020 7349 0888
www.christopherfarr.com

Christopher Farr
748 N. La Cienaga Boulevard
Los Angeles CA 90069, USA
+1 310 967 0064
www.christopherfarr.com

Felt
020 8772 0358
www.feltrugs.co.uk

Flor
116 N. York Road, Suite 300
Elmhurst, IL 60126, USA
+ 1 866 281 3567
support@flor.com
www.flor.com

IKEA
0845 355 1141
www.ikea.co.uk
www.ikea.com

Karastan
508 East Morris Street
Dalton, GA 307211, USA
+ 1 800 234 1120
karastan@rsvpcomm.com
www.karastan.com

The Natural Rug Store
0845 076 0086
www.naturalrugstore.co.uk

Roger Oates Floors & Fabrics
01531 632718
www.rogeroates.com

The Rug Company
124 Holland Park Avenue
London W11 4UE
020 7229 5148
4701 West Freeway, Suite 500
Fort Worth, TX 7610,7 USA
+1 817 738 7847
therugcompany.info
www.therugcompany.com

Rug Store
020 8876 0070
www.rugstore.org

Tufenkian Artisan Carpets
919 Third Avenue Ground Floor
New York, NY 10022, USA
+1 212 475 2475
www.tufenkiancarpets.com

Madeline Weinrib
ABC Carpet & Home
888 Broadway 6th Floor
New York, NY 10003, USA
+1 212 473 3000 x3780
contact@madelineweinrib.com
www.madelineweinrib.com

TILES
There are so many beautiful tiles to
choose from today but remember: you
have to live with them for a while so
take your time and choose wisely from
some of our favourites below.

Alstone
1080 Lousons Road
Union, NJ 07083
+ 1 800 255 7866
info@allstone.net
www.allstone.net

Ann Sacks
+1 800 278 8453
www.annsacks.com

Armstrong
2500 Columbia Ave.
P.O. Box 3001
Lancaster, PA 17604, USA
+1 717 397 0611
www.armstrong.com

B & Q
0845 609 6688
ww.diy.com

Bisazza
www.store.bisazzausa.com
info@bisazzausa.com

Cement Tiles
+1 877 886 0689
usacementtiles@mosaicdelsur.com
www.cement-tiles-usa.com

Collinson Ceramic & Porcelain Tiles
0131 313 3577
www.collinson-ceramics.co.uk

Coverings Etc
138 Spring Street, 6th Floor
New York, NY 10012, USA
+1 212 625 9393
www.coveringsetc.com

Criterion Tiles
020 7736 9610
www.criterion-tiles.co.uk

Crossville
P.O. Box 1168
Crossville, TN 38557, USA
+1 931 484 2110
samples@crossvilleinc.com
www.crossvilleinc.com

Discover Tile
1 Design Center Place #647
Boston, MA 02210,USA
+1 617 330 7900
inquiries@discovertile.com
www.discovertile.com

Dominic Crinson
Hothouse, 274 Richmond Road
London E8 3QW
020 7241 7467
info@crinson.com
www.crinson.com

Emery & Cie
020 8969 0222
www.emeryetcie.com

Fired Earth
Twyford Mill, Oxford Road
Adderbury, Oxfordshire OX17 3SX
Head office 01295 814 399
Stockists 0845 366 0400
www.firedearth.com

John Lewis
08456 049 049
www.johnlewis.co.uk

Marlborough Tiles
01672512422
www.malrboroughtiles.com

Mod Walls
800 Estates Dr, Suite 100
Aptos, CA 95003, USA
+1 877 439 9734
service@modwalls.com
www.modwalls.com

Porcelanosa
+34 964 507 140
grupo@porcelanosa.com
www.porcelanosa.com

Provenza
9731 Irvine Center Drive
Irvine, CA 92618, USA
+1 877 455 7890
support@provenzafloors.com
www.provenzafloors.com

Mosaic House
32 West 22nd Street
New York, NY 10010, USA
+1 212 414 2525
contactus@mosaichse.com
www.mosaichse.com

Tile Click
www.tileclick.co.uk

Tile Depot
0800 849 2120
www.thetiledepot.co.uk

Tile Heaven
01952 433094
www.tile-heaven.co.uk

Tile HQ
01782 597750
ww.tilehq.co.uk

Tex Tiles
01949 842515
www.tilesbytextiles.com

Topps Tiles
0800 023 4703
www.toppstiles.co.uk

Urban Archaeology
sales@urbanarchaeology.com
www.urbanarchaeology.com

Villa Lagoon Tile
15342 Fort Morgan Road
Gulf Shores, AL 36542, USA
+1 251 968 3375
info@VillaLagoonTile.com
www.villalagoontile.com

VINTAGE SOURCES
These markets are gems that you don't
want to miss because they've been
hand-picked by some of today's top
designers, who only source the best.

1st Dibs
www.1stdibs.com
On-line marketplace for antique and mid-
century modern furniture from America's
best dealers.

Abodeon
1731 Massachusetts Avenue,
Cambridge, MA 02138, USA
+1 617 497 0137
info@abodeon.com
www.abodeon.com
From mid-century furniture to
contemporary pendant lamps and
Scandinavian ceramics, this shop has a
little something for everyone.

After Noah
261 King's Road
London SW3 5EL
020 7359 4281
www.afternoah.com
Vintage homewares and furniture
including salvaged industrial lamps,
furniture and accessories.

Ark
9 Norfolk Street
Cambridge CB1 2LD
01223 307676
www.arkcambridge.co.uk
Vintage furniture, retro kitchenware,
lighting and children's toys.

Baileys Home Design
Whitecross Farm
Bridstow, Herefordshire HR9 6JU
01989 561931
www.baileyshomeandgarden.com
Rescued and recycled items from
abandoned bobbins to lamp bases, mirror
frames to tables plus locally sourced
pottery simple useful products.

Berry Red
29 Church Street
Hereford HR2 1LE
01432 274805
www.berryred.co.uk
Bright and beautiful homewares and
accessories from Greengate and others.

Caravan
3 Redchurch Street, London E2 7DJ
020 7033 3522
info@caravanstyle.com
www.caravanstyle.com
Owned by author and sought-after stylist
Emily Chalmers, Caravan showcases
hand-picked flea market finds and
vintage-inspired homewares and lighting
plus designers such as Deborah Bowness
(handpainted wallpaper) and Jieldé
(lamps).

City Vintage
13 Colinton Road
Edinburgh EH10 5DP
0131 446 3652
www.cityvintage.co.uk
Eclectic mix of vintage and retro furniture,
mirrors, antiques, collectables and vintage
jewellery.

COMINGHOME Interior
Lindener Marktplatz 5, 30449
Hannover, Germany
+ 49 511 2158196
info@cominghome-interior.de
www.cominghome-interior.de
One of Germany's largest dealers of
vintage design classics from furniture to
lighting and home decor with an inspiring
store and a larger nearby showroom and
warehouse. If they do not have it, they'll
find it for you.

Darr
369 Atlantic Avenue, Brooklyn,
NY 11217, USA
+1 718 797 9733
info@shopdarr.com
www.shopdarr.com
An eclectic store filled with found objects
and furniture.

Dee Puddy
01794 323020
www.deepuddy.co.uk
Vintage style home accessories and
genuine one-offs.

Dotty Moos Country Home Emporium
01380 840403
www.dottymoos.co.uk
Original and vintage style country
homewares.

Emma loves Retro
07930 521856
www.emmalovesretro.co.uk
Limited edition, handmade vintage fabric
cushions and accessories.

Fade Interiors
17 Oxford Street, Woodstock,
Oxfordshire OX20 1TH
01993 811655
www.fadeinteriors.com
Ever changing stock of handpainted
vintage furniture, restored old chairs and
decorative objects for house and garden.

Few and Far
242 Brompton Road
London SW3 2BB
020 7225 7070
shop@fewandfar.net
www.fewandfar.net
Vintage meets new in this curated
collection of décor and fashion from
producers and artisans worldwide.

Ici et la
7 Nickson Street, Surry Hills, Sydney
2010, Australia
+ 61 02 83991173
shop@icietla.com.au
www.icietla.com.au
Known for their vibrant striped fabrics,
garden furniture, French antiques and
canvas deckchairs.

In my Room
35 Gloucester Road
North Laine, Brighton
East Sussex BN1 4AQ
01273 675506
www.inmyroom.co.uk
Vintage 20th century furniture, post-war
and industrial design.

I Want Vintage
P O Box 8773
Coalville LE67 0BN
0845 053 3474
www.iwantvintage.co.uk
Virtual high street with links to specialist
vintage shops.

Izzi and Popo
258 Ferrars Street, South Melbourne,
Victoria, Australia 3205
+ 61 3 9696 1771
info@izziandpopo.com.au
izziandpopo.com.au
Imported antiques, second hand furniture
and European items for the home.

John Derian Company, Inc.
6 East 2nd Street, New York
NY 10003, USA
+1 212 677 3917
shop@johnderian.com
www.johnderian.com
Antique Moroccan trays and rugs, curious
collections of ceramics from Europe and
vintage and vintage-inspired accessories
and furniture from decoupage plates to
poufs.

Kit
18 High Street
Falmouth, Cornwall TR11 2AB
01326 218778
www.kitsboutique.com
Beautiful home accessories with a vintage
vibe.

Labour and Wait
18 Cheshire Street, London E2 6EH
+44 0 20 7729 6253
info@labourandwait.co.uk
www.labourandwait.co.uk
Simple timeless products, both vintage
and new, with a focus on functional
homewares with excellent craftsmanship.

Love Miss Daisy
07593 586 004
www.lovemissdaisy.com
Vintage clothing, accessories and
homewares.

Luna
139 Parliament Street
Nottingham NG1 1EE
0115 924 3267
www.luna-online.co.uk
1950s, 60s and 70s Objects and
Furniture for the home.

North Laine Antiques and Fleamarket
5–5a Upper Gardner Street
Brighton BN1 4AN
Large and varied collection of stalls
selling vintage furniture, homewares and
clothing.

Pale and Interesting
01797 344 077
www.paleandinteresting.com
The online boutique store of Atlanta Bartlett and Dave Coote that mixes timeworn and new furniture, handcrafted objects and fresh, functional accessories.

Paula Rubenstein Ltd.
65 Prince Street, New York
NY 10012, USA
+1 212 966 8954
American textiles from the nineteenth and twentieth centuries, lighting, home décor and rare antique industrial furniture.

The Peanut Vendor
133 Newington Green Road
London N1 4RA
020 7226 5727
www.thepeanutvendor.co.uk
Vintage furniture shop selling eclectic pieces and stylish classics, from Ercol furniture to quirky oddities.

Pigeon Vintage Furniture
1a Pelham Street
Brighton BN 4FA
07930 357362
www.pigeonvintage.co.uk
Vintage industrial furniture from desks and lamps to storage solutions, lighting and mirrors.

Planet Vintage Girl
252 Chester Road
Manchester M15 4EX
0161 839 5525
www.planetvintagegirl.com
British and American 20th-Century modern design.

Radio Days
87 Lower Marsh
London SE1 7AB
020 7928 0800
www.radiodaysvintage.co.uk
Vintage radios, ceramics and telephones.

RE
Bishops Yard, Main Street
Corbridge, Northumberland NE45 5LA
01434 634567
www.re-foundobjects.com
Unique range of RE-designed textiles and homewares, plus recycled, rescued and restored items.

Red Chair Antiques
14 Depot Street
Peterborough NH, 03458, USA
+1 603 924 5953
antiques@redchair-antiques.com
www.redchair-antiques.com
A gorgeous shop overflowing with vintage and antique things from French linen to monogrammed bedding, European furniture, fabric, trim, buttons.

RetroSixty
07841 535 864
www.retrosixty.co.uk
20th century American and Danish furniture from the 1950s to the 1970s.

Retrouvius.com
020 8960 6060
www.retrouvius.com
Architectural salvage, vintage furniture and home design.

Salvo
020 8400 6222
www.salvo.co.uk
Directory of UK and US architectural salvage and antiques dealers.

The Society, Inc.
18 Stewart Street, Paddington,
Australia NSW 2021
+61 2 9331 1592
sibella@thesocietyinc.com.au
www.thesocietyinc.com.au
Old haberdashery meets hardware store that specializes in textiles, paint, hardware, homewares, furniture and beautiful collections of things owned by stylist and author Sibella Court.

Source Antiques
Victoria Park Business Centre
Midland Road, Bath BA1 3AX
01225 469200
www.source-antiques.co.uk
20th century antiques, architectural salvage, lighting and garden items plus English Rose and Paul Metalcraft kitchens.

Swarm
31 (0) 6 44 035 637
l.oschman@chello.nl
www.swarmhome.com
Reclaimed objects made new using mostly vintage paintings and flea market finds, sold in Anthropologie stores worldwide and also available to commission directly from Swarm.

Take Me Home
07976 645 631
www.take-me-home.co.uk
Brighton-based supplier of vintage furniture, including cabinets, desks and dining suites in rosewood and teak plus leather sofas and ceramics from 1950s-1970s.

Three Potato Four
376 Shurs Lane, Bldg A
Philadelphia, PA 19128, USA
+1 267 335 3633
info@threepotatofourshop.com
www.threepotatofourshop.com
A delightful collection of mostly vintage finds available both in-store and online.

The Vintage Emporium
14 Bacon Street
Brick Lane
London E1 6CF
www.vintageemporiumcafe.com
Store specializing in vintage furniture and homewares.

Urban Village & General Stores
The Custard Factory
Gibb Street, Digbeth
Birmingham B9 4AA
0121 224 7367
www.urban-village.co.uk
Clothing, furniture, artwork and vintage vinyl from the 1950s-1970s.

Vinegar Hill
16 Milsom Street
Bath, Somerset BA1 1DE
01225 339498
www.vinegarhill.co.uk
Vintage and country style furniture and homewares.

Vintage Fair
www.vintagefair.co.uk
Listings of UK vintage fairs selling affordable vintage clothing, homewares and accessories.

Vintage Home
01367 718993
www.vintage-home.co.uk
Beautiful floral textiles and curtains, eiderdowns and quilts plus homewares.

WALLPAPER
Prints and patterns for the ceiling, walls, or to dress up the interior of a closet, these wallpaper selections range from bespoke to retro.

Abigail Borg
07793 033922
contact@abigailborg.co.uk
www.abigailborg.co.uk

Aimée Wilder
support@aimeewilder.com
www.aimeewilder.com

Anna French
020 7737 6555
+1 800 379 6587
enquiries@annafrench.co.uk
www.annafrench.co.uk

Ann McGuire Studio
+1 570 595 3360
info@annmcguirestudio.com
www.annmcguirestudio.com

Anthropologie
020 7529 9800
www.anthropologie.co.uk

AphroChic
www.aphrochicshop.com

B & Q
0845 609 6688
www.diy.com

Bholu
+61 2 9698 0153
+1 310 897 1020 or +1 415 831 8809
australia@bholu.com
europe@bholu.com
usaeast@bholu.com or usawest@bholu.com
www.bholu.com

Brian Yates
01524 35035
sales@brian-yates.co.uk
www.brian-yates.co.uk

Cath Kidston
08450 262 440
www.cathkidston.co.uk

Cavern
+1 718 766 5464
inquires@cavernhome.com
www.cavernhome.com

Claire Coles
claire@clairecolesdesign.co.uk
www.clairecolesdesign.co.uk

Cole & Son
020 7376 4628
www.cole-and-son.com

Colefax & Fowler
020 7244 7427
www.colefax.com

Curiousa & Curiousa
0789 4423 250
www.curiousaandcuriousa.co.uk

Deborah Bowness
01757 248 500
deb@deborahbowness.com
www.deborahbowness.com

de Gournay
020 7352 9988
+1 212 564 9750
www.degournay.com

Designers Guild
020 7893 7400
info@designersguild.com
www.designersguild.com

Eijffinger
+31 (0)79 3441200
www.eijffinger.com

Elli Popp
info@ellipopp.com
+44 (0) 7957135041
www.ellipopp.com

Erica Wakerly
info@printpattern.com
+44 (0) 7940 577620
www.printpattern.com

Farrow & Ball
01202 876141
www.farrow-ball.com

Ferm Living
+45 7022 7523
+1 415 318 6412
info@ferm-living.com
www.ferm-living.com

Flavor Paper
+1 718 422 0230
info@flavorleague.com
www.flavorleague.com

Florence Broadhurst
www.signatureprints.com.au

F. Schumacher & Co.
+1 800 523 1200
info@fsco.com
www.fschumacher.com

Graham & Brown
0800 328 8452
help.is@grahambrown.com
www.grahambrown.com

Greg Kinsella
020 7352 7989
www.gregkinsella.com

Grow House Grow
+1 770 883 2709
info@growhousegrow.com
www.growhousegrow.com

Harlequin
0845 126 5570
www.harlequin.uk.com

Homebase
www.homebase.co.uk

Hygge & West
+1 888 784 3632
info@hyggeandwestshop.com
www.hyggeandwestshop.com

ISAK
info@isak.co.uk
www.isak.co.uk

JAB ANSTOETZ
JABverkauf@jab.de
www.jab.de

Jill Malek
+1 718 207 9587
jill@jillmalek.com
www.jillmalek.com

Jocelyn Warner
020 7375 3754
madeleine@jocelynwarner.com
www.jocelynwarner.com

Laura Ashley
0871 230 2301
www.lauraashley.co.uk

Lene Toni Kjeld
+45 6170 6856
ltk@walldecoration.dk
www.walldecoration.dk

Liberty
Regent Street
London W1B 5AH
020 7734 1234
www.liberty.co.uk

Lisa Bengtsson
+ 46 70 57 99 345
kontakt@lisabengtsson.se
www.lisabengtsson.se

Lizzie Allen
07947 474928
lizzie@lizzieallen.co.uk
www.lizzieallen.co.uk

Louise Body
07734 907357
louise@louisebodywallprint.com
www.louisebody.com

Madison & Grow
+1 323 522 6683
info@madisonandgrow.com
www.madisonandgrow.com

Mimou
+46 457 19070
info@mimou.se
www.mimou.se

MissPrint
020 8470 7896
contact@MissPrint.co.uk
www.missprint.co.uk

Mod Green Pod
+1 512 524 5196
info@modgreenpod.com
www.modgreenpod.com

Mulberry Home
020 7352 3173
www.mulberryhome.com

Nama Rococo
+1 413 652 2312
info@namarococo.com
www.namarococo.com

Neisha Crosland
020 7978 4389
sales@turnellandgigon.com
www.neishacrosland.com

Next
0844 844 8333
www.next.co.uk

Nina Campbell
020 7225 1011
www.ninacampbell.com

Nobilis
www.nobiliswallpaper.com

Orla Kiely
020 8720 1117
www.orlakiely.com

Osborne & Little
020 8812 3000
+1 203 359 1500
oandl@osborneandlittle.com
www.osborneandlittle.com

Onszelf
info@onszelf.com
www.onszelf.com

Palacepapers
+1 773 551 5710
www.palacepapers.com

PaperBoy
020 7193 9135
enquiries@paperboywallpaper.co.uk
www.paperboywallpaper.co.uk

Paper Mills
+1 718 552 6663
info@papermills.net
www.papermills.net

Pattern Tales
07921 837 847
hello@patterntales.com
www.patterntales.com

PiP Studio
+31 343 475 598
www.pipstudio.com

Publisher Textiles
+61 2 9569 6044
info@publishertextiles.com.au
www.publishertextiles.com.au

P van b
+49 30 44 35 61 05
info@pvanb.com
www.pvanb.com

Robert Kime
07229 0886
www.robertkime.com

Romo
08456 444400
+49 89 89666160
verkauf@romo.de
sales@romo.com
www.romo.de
www.romofabrics.co.uk

Rose & Grey
0560 311 3405
www.roseandgrey.co.uk

Sanderson
0844 543 4749
www.sanderson-uk.com

Selfridges
0800 123 400
www.selfridges.co.uk

Six Hands
+61 2 9310 5225
hello@sixhands.com.au
www.sixhands.com.au

Studio Ditte
+31 (0)6 27 02 01 04
mail@studioditte.nl
www.studioditte.nl

Studio Nommo
info@studionommo.com
www.studionommo.com

Surface View
0118 922 1327
info@surfaceview.co.uk
www.surfaceview.co.uk

Totally Home
0800 376 9779
www.totallyhome.co.uk

Tracy Kendall
+44 (0) 207 640 9071
info@tracykendall.com
www.tracykendall.com

Turner Pocock
020 7603 3440
info@turnerpocockcazalet.co.uk
www.turnerpocockcazalet.co.uk

TapetenAgentur
info@tapetenagentur.de
www.tapetenagentur.de

Timorous Beasties
020 7833 5010
info@timorousbeasties.com
www.timorousbeasties.com

Voyage Decoration
0141 641 1700
info@voyfab.co.uk
www.voyagedecoration.com

Wallpaper Direct
01323 4308886
www.wallpaperdirect.co.uk

York Wallcoverings
+1 717 846 4456
www.yorkwall.com

Zoffany
0844 543 4600
enquiries@zoffany.uk.com
www.zoffany.com

BLOGS WE LIKE

Here is an inspirational list of decorating blogs that we suggest tuning into in addition to the bloggers quoted throughout this book listed in our directory. See which one has a style that you're attracted to and enjoy their beautiful finds.

www.afieldjournal.blogspot.com

www.thebedlamofbeefy.blogspot.com

www.blackeiffel.blogspot.com

www.brightbazaar.blogspot.com

www.chezlarsson.com

www.cocokelley.blogspot.com

www.creaturecomfortsblog.com

www.designevolutionblog.com

www.designformankind.com

www.designismine.blogspot.com

www.desiretoinspire.net

www.design-milk.com

www.designspongeonline.com

www.dottieangel.blogspot.com

www.emmas.blogg.se

www.habituallychic.blogspot.com

www.inkandwit.blogspot.com

www.madebygirl.blogspot.com

www.mloves.typepad.com

www.ohhellofriendblog.com

www.ohjoy.blogs.com

www.plushpalate.blogspot.com

www.poppytalk.blogspot.com

www.swiss-miss.com

www.annesage.com

www.thedesignfiles.net

www.theselby.com

www.simplygrove.com

www.stylecourt.blogspot.com

www.thehappyhomeblog.com

www.younghouselove.com

You can find more amazing blogs to peruse at your leisure here:
www.decor8blog.com

ACKNOWLEDGEMENTS & AFTERWORD

I'm enormously grateful to my fantastic readers who follow *decor8* so loyally. You've helped make my dream of authoring a book possible and I feel deeply touched and honoured to have your support and friendship.

Debi Treloar – Your focus, amazing eye, infectious laugh and late night chats made this project run so beautifully. Thank you for consistently taking such 'awesome' photos. A special thanks to Woody Holding for helping us so much on shoots, too.

Jacqui Small – Thank you for such a wonderful opportunity. You are fair, kind and patient and I admire your dedication and wisdom. A warm thanks to Joanna Copestick for pulling me in on this project and for your beautiful words and overall lovely spirit. Sian Parkhouse, thank you for your eloquent editing and patience, you magically made it all come together. To our book designer Robin Rout – you had many cooks in your kitchen yet you managed to pull off a book that satisfied us all. Bravo! Kerenza Swift and Clare Limpus, thank you both for your dedication and attention to detail. It's been a joy to collaborate with such a professional, organized team! I'd also like to thank Chronicle Books – I am honoured to be part of your line-up of authors. Rebecca Friedman – you are the best agent anyone could ever hope to have, you are a star!

Thanks to the lovely contributors in this book for opening your doors and to Leslie Shewring – I am so happy to call you my friend.

A big hug and lots of love to my dear mother Christine, you encouraged me since I was very young to write and decorate and you were right. A mother always knows best!

To my husband Thorsten Becker, thank you for your warmth, guidance, support and wisdom throughout this project and long before – you always encouraged me to pursue my passions with confidence which resulted in my blog and now this book. You have given me the best years of my life, I love you so much!

Holly Becker

A big thank you to Jacqui Small who thought it was a good idea in the first place and for her encouragement, wisdom and more than a few working lunches; Holly Becker, partner-in-crime, for her globetrotting locations and boundless enthusiasm; Debi Treloar for her beautiful photography; Sian Parkhouse for her ever-efficient, good-humoured editing and schedule watching; Kerenza Swift for keeping us all in shape and Robin Rout, for ongoing consultancy on the world's best fish and chips in the face of late-night design deadlines. To Hannah, Julia and the lovely Nige for putting up with my time-consuming relationship with the computer.

Joanna Copestick

'Think laterally – a beautiful but old teapot with a broken spout could make a great vase, a distressed wobbly stool could become a plant stand, a lace bed cover could hang at the window, a relatively small length of fabric could cover a panel of a screen.'

Emily Chalmers, stylist

'Casually place all the things you love the most on the shelf without thinking too much about them. Stand back, and then remove items that are not working well within the display. For me it's always about allowing things to flow – like a story, really.'

Pia Jane Bijkerk, stylist

'Start somewhere; start small. Pick one room to tackle. There are no mistakes that can't be undone.'

Annette Tatum, textile designer/author

Before you close this book, we simply must share a few more tips, beginning with what we feel is the most important: decorating should be fun!

Allow your creativity to flow, do your research and be observant to your surroundings, yet be careful not to over-think things or you could suffer from analysis-paralysis and the sofa will sit in the middle of an empty room for months! Another word of advice that we have found to be most helpful is to not decorate for someone else – it's your home, follow your gut instincts and create your own style.

Remember too, when it comes to decorating there is no end point. Your home evolves along with you and your family so be comforted by the thought that you don't have to rush through your plans – enjoy the process. And a final bit of advice: create a mood in your home that pleases all of the senses – sight, touch, sound, taste, scent. A batch of freshly baked cookies, a cosy cableknit throw, a chat around the table with a good friend – these things matter as much as a good floor plan or a carefully selected sofa, so make time for special moments in your home.

We hope that you have enjoyed *Decorate*. It is our fondest wish that this book will become a friend to you when you're in need of inspiring words and imagery, as you go forth to create a home that you can put your personal stamp on and enjoy for years to come.

Warm regards,

Holly & Joanna

CARDIFF
COUNCIL

05093032

A & H

2017

£25.00

5540236

"You can tell **A LOT** about a **person** by how they shape **their home** – about the colours they choose the patterns they layer and what lines their walls.

Shannon Fricke "